ABANDONED IMAGES

ABANDONED IMAGES

FILM AND FILM'S END

Stephen Barber

REAKTION BOOKS

Published by Reaktion Books Ltd
33 Great Sutton Street
London ECIV ODX, UK

First published 2010

Printed and bound in Great Britain
by CPI Antony Rowe, Chippenham, Wiltshire

British Library Cataloguing in Publication Data
Barber, Stephen, 1961–
    Abandoned images : film and film's end.
    1. Motion picture theaters – California – Los Angeles – History.
    2. Motion picture theaters – California – Los Angeles – Remodeling for
    other use.
    3. Motion picture audiences – Attitudes.
    4. Motion pictures – Social aspects.
    I. Title
    302.2'343'0905-dc22

ISBN: 978 1 86189 645 2

CONTENTS

INTRODUCTION

The nature and status of film are undergoing a profound transformation, which will undoubtedly lead to the perception of film
itself being formulated in new ways, and to films being created or re-
imagined with unprecedented aims. Similarly, cinematic space is also
experiencing fundamental shifts, notably in the abandonment of its
distinctive forms. Since the centenary in 1995 of the first film projections for public audiences, and during the subsequent rise and
expansion of the digital era, multiple predictions of 'the end' of
film have made made. Although it still possesses a formidable
industrial presence, film, in many ways, has lost its unique status
within the multiple media of corporations, and become an abandoned
entity, formed of abandoned images. At the same time, film appears
an ineradicable presence that vivifies memory, overhauls architecture,
and engages in an intricate and intensive confrontation with the
human eye. Film also holds its own approaches to sensory self-
abandonment, and its particular, strategic formulations of 'the end'.
This book probes the dynamics of film at a pivotal moment in its
history, when it may either disappear into the engulfing forms of
digital-media industries, or else be reconfigured, by its infiltration
into new forms of human vision. Above all, the book examines and
visualizes conceptions of the 'abandonment' of film, and its wide-
ranging implications, by scrutinizing (and inhabiting) in depth a

revealing terrain of cinematic abandonment: the Broadway avenue of twelve ruined cinemas, once grandiose and excessive, now derelict but intact, in downtown Los Angeles, which offer their extraordinary facades and interiors as screens for the exploration of film's end.[1]

This book consists of four parts, each of which interrogates different, but interconnected, elements of film and cinematic space, and their relationship to ideas of abandonment and termination. The first part is concerned with film theorists and cultural historians who have, in a range of ways, formulated 'ends' of film, and also with filmmakers whose work involves an anatomizing of decay and ruination, often by making explicit links to corporeal and memorial processes of disintegration, or whose work, as with that of Michelangelo Antonioni, invokes the 'terminal' or extreme landscapes and environments within which film must operate, in order to maximally seize its own capacity to dissect human acts and forms. This part of the book also initiates an exploration of the cinematic space of Los Angeles's Broadway, examining its diverse layers of abandonment, which can disclose evocative filmic detritus, notably when that space is re-inhabited, in its dereliction, by films preoccupied with sensory falls and hauntings, as in the work of David Lynch. This part of the book also examines how film's apparent disintegration and obsolescence contrarily entail the originating of compulsive reinventions, with sensorial and ocular dimensions, of film and its spaces.

The second part of the book looks specifically at how film images, across filmic history, appeared complicit with their own decay and downfall, and how that content relates to conceptions of film as comprising a sensitized medium for human memory and history, and for the determining of the particular forms of the gestures, behaviours and dreams of its vast audiences. The memory of film remains so embedded within the nature of memory itself that the 'lapsing', shattering or disappearance of film constitutes a significant trauma of memory, within a contemporary era that predominantly formulates visual media of oblivion. Often, film has been charged with holding and displaying images of death – as in such documentary films as *Africa Addio* and *Gimme Shelter* – and of prefiguring terminal or apocalyptic events, as though film formed the supreme medium for the embodiment of definitive human endings. This part of the book also examines what happens to cinematic space after its distinctive presence and aura appear to be erased, when a cinema becomes abandoned or demolished, or re-used for seemingly antithetical and alien purposes to that of film projection. Cinematic space may be overhauled, or else entirely uprooted and displaced, as in the iconic architecture of the Hollywood and Vine metro station in Los Angeles, which re-creates the aura of a lavish cinema. In all cases, the residual traces of film, notably those which appear to intimate its end, constitute vital materials for the instigation of new visual forms.

The third part of the book examines, in particular, the relationship between film and the human eye, and the future of that rapport as film's status is transformed. Notably in the 1920s, filmmakers such as Dziga Vertov and Luis Buñuel conceived of the eye as a target for film's experiments, with the aim of creating actively engaged spectators. Throughout the subsequent decades, that often-confrontational relationship between the eye and film has been an insightful one, in determining the parameters of how film impacts upon its spectators and its surroundings; film has been conceived as entailing and presenting conflagrations and woundings, transmitted from the eye to film, or from film to the eye. Film has frequently envisaged acts of blinding, and the loss or ending of vision. Cinematic space, in the forms of the lavish film-palaces constructed worldwide in the 1920s and '30s, indicates another dimension of that rapport between film and the eye, in the architectural formulation of an excessive ocular luxury which could serve to divert the spectator's eye away from film, to scan the multiple attractions of cinemas' interiors and facades; the ruination or abandonment of such spaces now entails a form of austerity in which that luxurious engulfing of the eye is abruptly ripped away, thereby instigating new perceptions and formulations of vision.

The final part of the book probes in detail what forms of media may take on film's powerful, often perverse obsessions in the future. Film's survival in the digital era is bound to the way in which it enduringly constituted the axis of sensory and ocular experiences, which became so central to human perception, over an extended period, that film may, finally, be able to transmutate into all future media that attempt to seize, beguile and assault the human eye. Especially in an era of digital malfunctions and crashes, the residue of film – its material once held together for projection by splices – may be crucial for the reparatory suturing of memory and vision. Architecture itself may be determined by film's disappearance, and be required to work to conjure film back into existence, in a parallel way to that in which film's pioneers of the 1880s and '90s used magical sleights of the eye to bring film into being, and foresaw ways, in the face of what then appeared to be impossible technological obstacles, to project film's images to its audiences. The contemporary space of abandoned cinemas now appears as that of an experimental laboratory for the conception of new media of human vision; the book ends with a resuscitatory act of filmic projection in an otherwise abandoned cinema, intimating that film remains an essential, aberrant spectacle.

PART 1

FILM AND THE END

Los Angeles Broadway 1

Film's end begins with a glorious scar on the face of the city. Once the end of film has been located, the eye can travel in any direction, backwards in time, forwards in time, or more profoundly into a moment of immediacy, and into the transformative space and corporeality of filmic ruination. Film's end is a matter for the human eye, for memory, and oblivion.

The Broadway avenue of downtown Los Angeles holds the greatest concentration worldwide of abandoned, but intact, cinemas, whose histories encompass almost the entirety of the existence of film, together with its obsessions, caprices and mutations. That procession of once-lavish and luxurious cinemas, the zenith of technological innovation in their respective moments of construction, along the Broadway avenue, forms a geographically linear graveyard in which to experience film's end, running directly north to south. The parallel westerly avenues carry innumerable corporate image-screens (the digitally animated advertising surfaces that became pervasive in cities worldwide in the early 2000s, fluctuating in scale from the size of an entire building's facade to that of a minuscule display screen) and highrise banking towers, while the adjacent easterly avenues contain archaic, century-old skid-row hotels and now-illegible, tea-painted hoardings for long-gone

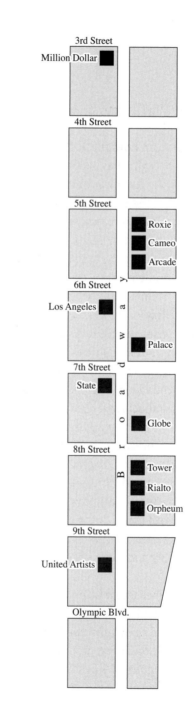

companies, inscribed directly onto the upper storeys of the buildings' walls.

Filmic history can now only exist in fragments, since its amalgamation with the digital has irreparably scrambled its resolution, but also because film itself was never a medium to be incorporated and defused within the linear, the historical, the categorical, and always wielded an integral capacity for aberrance, for the arbitrary and for the shattering of time. Even in their geographical existence, the cinemas contained in the linear north–south avenue of Broadway possess contradictory histories, multiple origins and ends, as well as disparate architectures, facades and interiors. In most cities worldwide, a collection of grandiose cinemas such as those of Broadway, once obsolete and emptied out, would have been demolished, as happened in many cities, such as San Francisco, Tokyo and London, so that such cinemas' presence, and its deep embedding in the lives and visions of those cities' populations, would have to be conjured or hallucinated back into existence, or substantiated with photographic and memory-based evidence, in order for that once-seminal aura of cinema to even subsist in the contemporary moment. By contrast, in Los Angeles's Broadway – in large part through the power of indifference and oblivion itself, exercised in what, for decades, was a near-forgotten and neglected zone of the city – the abandoned cinemas perversely survived, as they did in the avenues of other cities, such as Lisbon and Riga, thereby tangibly embodying, in their contrary dereliction and endurance, the living end of film.

From the northernmost point of Los Angeles's Broadway, the twelve cinemas extend down the avenue as an astonishing litany of names emblazoned on dilapidated but still-prominent marquees and signs: the Million Dollar Theater, the Roxie, the Cameo, the Arcade, the Los Angeles Theater, the Palace, the State, the Globe, the Tower, the Rialto, the Orpheum and the United Artists Theater.

Several of them were originally named after the cinema entrepreneurs who built them (Alexander Pantages, William H. Clune),
and acquired their later names once those entrepreneurs had
vanished into obscurity or bankruptcy. Most of the cinemas are constellated in small groups, alongside or opposite one another, with
the Million Dollar Theater and the United Artists Theater, at the
extreme ends of the avenue, stranded at a block or two's distance
from the others. The cinemas of Broadway were all constructed
between 1910 and 1931, with the first and last cinemas (the Cameo
and the Roxie) positioned directly alongside one another. During
those two decades of the cinemas' pre-eminence, Los Angeles's film
premieres and first runs of major films often took place in Broadway, and the night-time avenues became saturated with crowds
awaiting the arrival of searchlight-illuminated film stars. That interval of two decades, its origin only fifteen years on from the first
ever public film screenings, in 1895, and its ending seventy years
or so in advance of the engulfing onset of the digital era, around
the year 2000, is a moment stranded within competing film histories; those histories left the Broadway cinemas marooned within the
city's space, once the onrush of Los Angeles's film industry had
transplanted its axis westwards, towards Hollywood, at the beginning of the 1930s (extending a trajectory that had already propelled
that axis from a transitory origin two avenues eastwards, in Main
Street, site of Los Angeles's ramshackle and ephemeral nickelodeons). As a result, the cinemas of Broadway remained within their
own cracked fragment of history, and their own scorched-earth
urban terrain.

The facades and interiors of the Broadway cinemas were designed to transmit infinite luxury and maximal expense to the eyes
of their audiences; that excessive expense could even serve to
name the cinemas, as with the avenue's northernmost cinema, the
Million Dollar Theater. In many cases, shopping arcades and office

Los Angeles Theater foyer (fragment).

complexes were incorporated into the architectural design, either surrounding the cinema's auditorium or else extending several storeys above it. The cinemas' exterior design relentlessly propelled their audience's eyes into the interiors, beginning with the vividly coloured solar mosaics embedded into the public sidewalks in front of the foyers. The facades, often constructed with premium-quality stone imported from Italian quarries, and intricately carved and decorated with figures drawn from European or Mayan mythologies, both exclaimed the titles of current films on colossal marquees and hoardings, and intimated that the film-going experience was to be a lavish, cultured one. Each foyer accentuated that extravagance, with opulent decoration replicating Versailles palace interiors or Gothic infernos, and led to marbled restrooms, restaurants, walnut-panelled smoking-lounges and sound-proofed areas in which to exile wailing children. The projection-box contained the latest image technology, and the entire building demonstrated techno-logical innovations, including systems to transmit the film image onto miniaturized screens for the socializing audience seated in the lounge areas. Inside the auditorium itself, often able to seat several thousand spectators in multiple tiers, balconies and side-boxes, the audience first saw the spectacular fire curtain, emblazoned with sunbursts or planetary constellations, before the vast screen was re-vealed and the film began.

The cinemas had been constructed so that their own eventual disintegration and ruination would form an equally compelling ocular and sensorial spectacle to their originating moment of glory. In some cases, the moments of their completion and redundancy were near simultaneous; the Los Angeles Theater, constructed as the venue for the premiere of Chaplin's *City Lights* in January 1931 (Chaplin arrived in Broadway with Albert Einstein, in front of Depression-era crowds forming hostile bread-queues rather than an entranced audience), had gone bankrupt by the end of the same year. New cinemas, such as the Chinese Theater and the El Capitan Theater, had already been built on Hollywood Boulevard, and now supplanted those on Broadway as the film industry's preferred ven-ues. Each of the twelve Broadway cinemas passed through the following five decades in different ways, with some cinemas packed beyond capacity, 24 hours a day, during the war years of 1941–5, for cut-price screenings of B-movies and newsreels. The avenue's department stores, which had formed another point of attraction for its cinemas' audiences, declined over the postwar decades, leaving empty buildings, and a huge influx of Mexican and El Sal-vadorian street-traders led to many cinemas specializing in South American films, before spiralling downwards into an array of martial arts and exploitation genres. By the late 1970s and into the '80s, Broadway had become a forbidding part of the city at night, with few people remaining in the streets after dark other than the mad, desperate and homeless; at times, otherwise-homeless people literally lived in the never-closing cinemas. All-night screenings for riotous audiences of cult-film die-hards left the cinemas' original screens indented by thrown missiles, torn and stained; several cinemas supplemented their film-screenings with one-off performances by the era's punk bands. One cinema, the Rialto, was closed down since its construction no longer met earthquake regulations, but in most cases, the cinemas ended in pornography, with depleted audiences transfixed by images of pornography stars spraying semen on

Million Dollar Theater tower (fragment).

Decasia, 2002.

the already stained screens. By the early 1990s, all had ceased showing films, taking on their new status as abandoned cinemas.

The transformation of the Broadway cinemas by their abandonment reveals how those ghost-spaces retain the aura of film and
accentuate it into a vital matter of memory and destruction, and how
those spaces enable the prising-apart of filmic obsession, to show
both its seminal power and the power of its disintegration. The posthumous mutation of those cinemas since their closures – into cultist
churches, nightclubs, sex venues, experimental art spaces, shop-
storerooms for plasma televisions and digital artefacts, or simply into
petrified spaces of accumulated ruination – also illuminates how
film, with its ongoing, hybrid mutations, even after its ostensible
'death', remains the pivotal medium for human experience and for
its new forms of vision.

Approaching Broadway from the north, the first element to be
seen of those cinemas' traces, rising above the adjacent buildings,
is the summit of the office tower built above the Million Dollar
Theater, imprinted with the date of its construction, 1918 – and
once occupied by William Mulholland, the legendary bringer of
water via aqueducts to the newly developing city of Los Angeles,
and a figure demonized as an incestuous and immoral criminal

by Roman Polanski, as his fictional character Noah Cross, in the 1974 film *Chinatown*, whose narrative castigates the very origin and means of creation of the film-megalopolis of Los Angeles.

Anatomizing Cinema's Death

Film has had so many ends, so many deaths, that an objective observer of the medium (an omniscient and dispassionate onlooker from another time, like those observing the visions of the human species in Chris Marker's film *La Jetée*) might conclude that its pioneers of the 1880s and '90s had created it purely in order to have the perverse pleasure of killing it, or of watching as its materials deteriorated, and its spaces became abandoned. One of the great advocates of the death of cinema, the film archivist Paulo Cherchi Usai, wrote of how the digital era formed an antithetical and non-aligned presence to that of film, and that the vital work of the film archivist was now to observe and record the intricate processes of decay which manifested film's disintegration, as the nitro-cellulose base of the material used in cinema's early decades gradually returned to its constituent elements: nitric acid, camphor and cotton: 'The ultimate goal of film history is an account of its own disappearance, or its transformation into another entity.'[1] The digital theorist Lev Manovich has observed a comparable process of decay in the digital image data that has superseded film, noting that 'while in theory, computer technology entails the flawless replication of data, its actual use in contemporary society is characterised by loss of data, degradation, and noise.'[2] Usai also makes this parallel between the processes of decay which unite two otherwise irreconcilable media, the filmic and the digital: 'As soon as it is deposited on a matrix, the digital image is subject to a similar destiny; its causes may be different, but the effects are the same.'[3] The digital image is as precarious and fragile an entity as that of film, additionally exposed (unlike film) to the permanent possibility of a technological meltdown or digital crash engendered by social instability or human caprice; but the digital image's death remains a new and unknown one, while film possesses a long history of ends.

The fascination which abandoned, ruined and expiring cinemas exert upon filmmakers worldwide is evident in numerous films located in such spaces, such as Tsai Ming-Liang's *Goodbye, Dragon Inn* (2003), Wim Wenders's *Lisbon Story* (1994) and Theo Angelopoulos's *The Beekeeper* (1986); such films often explore and foreground the space of the decrepit cinema's projection-box as the pre-eminent, revelatory site of film's abandonment. That fascination with terminal cinematic space forms a variant of a compelling filmic preoccupation with envisaging and probing its own decay and erasure. And like the work of dissection performed by an anatomist, the close observer of film's end is working on corporeal as well as visual materials. The filmmaker Bill Morrison made an explicit alliance between the decay of film and the decay of the human body in his 2002 film *Decasia*, whose production consisted of literally filming the disintegration of film, in the form of sequences from documentary and fiction films which had deteriorated in the archives in which they were stored, so that the human bodies held in those sequences now distort, deliquesce, vanish, suffer total erasure, exude ghostly ectoplasm, before abruptly resuscitating themselves, apparently miraculously, whenever the process of decay has affected only a limited sequence of film-footage. Morrison notes that: 'Like the film, our bodies will eventually be reduced to what essentially forms us. What they contain is who we are: our thoughts, dreams and memories.'[4] The end of film, then, may possess an aberrant narrative twist, entailing a liberatory unleashing, in which an interrogative viewing of the process of decay or abandonment undergone by film's images (reels confined to decay in film-cans),

Decasia, 2002.

or film's spaces (cinemas that have been abandoned), finally releases those incendiary charges of memory and dreaming that Morrison observes, now in a sensorial and ocular form intensified by their confinement within the space and time of filmic death, so that they emerge mutated and transformed, with new impacts for the human eye.

Announcers of the death of film have often pinpointed particular moments for that terminal event: moments often determined by preoccupations with time or technology. Purists who prefer film as silent (or as combined only with music) have vilified the coming of sound, and especially of a synchronized vocal dimension, to film's industries at the end of the 1920s, as marking that falling-away point, and with it the closure of a period of sustained experimentation with the film image, that had already been taken to a state of inventive extremity in F. W. Murnau's film *Sunrise* (1927), in Dziga Vertov's *Man with a Movie Camera* (1928) or in Luis Buñuel's *Un Chien Andalou* (1929), and that could have been taken further, if film had maintained its silence. Other moments of perceived film-death constellate the subsequent history of cinema, gathering momentum towards the end of the twentieth century. For filmmakers who began to see the potential for digital image-making as a creative strategy, the early 1990s marked a moment when it appeared that film could now be technologically surpassed by an exciting new medium which – at that moment, before the engulfing digitization of everyday life that had taken hold by the end of that same decade – would constitute a natural transition onwards from the filmic medium; filmmakers such as Peter Greenaway and Wim Wenders presented their films of that era, *Prospero's Books* (1991) and *Until the End of the World* (1991), as embodying the way in which the digital image could carry every visual texture and resonance that film had, but in an infinitely enhanced and expansive way. A further moment of film's announced end came in 1995–6, at the time of the centenary of the first film screenings for a paying audience, held by the German film-pioneers Max and Emil Skladanowsky at the Wintergarten Ballroom in Berlin on 1 November 1895, and the subsequent public screenings by the French film pioneers Auguste and Louis Lumière in Paris. That variant on the death of film assumed that the medium had possessed a finite lifespan: one hundred years, to the second, as though the first moment of projection at the Wintergarten Ballroom marked its origin, and the winding-down of the film-reels' revolutions at a screening a century later marked its demise. The film theorist Laura Mulvey noted the engrained preoccupation with death in film, and the speed or stilling of film-projection that is integral to the mediation of filmic death, in her book *Death 24x a Second*. She proposed that the years following 2000 also marked another of film's deaths, since the momentum of the digital era's ascendancy across the 1990s appeared increasingly intent on obliterating film entirely, and also because the years following film's centenary had seen the disappearances of seminal film icons such as Marlon Brando: 'As time passes, the ghosts crowd around the cinema as its own life lies in question and the years around the centenary saw the death of the last great Hollywood stars.'[5] Film now became something that viewers were attracted to, if they wanted to see the presence of death at work: a presence habitually voided from the digital image. But if film revealed death, or the imminence of death, that capacity had already emerged within its earliest moments, since one of the first ever filmic sequences, shot by Louis Le Prince in 1888, had recorded an elderly relative days before her death, in a garden in the city of Leeds, and if Le Prince had been able to project the images he had shot (a technological impossibility at that moment, and for the next seven years), his audience would have seen the first film images that actively mediated death. In defiance of its multiply announced occurrences, the death of film really begins with its originating images.

In 1877, eleven years before Le Prince shot the first film images, and eighteen years before the first film screenings for public audiences, the inventor Eadweard Muybridge was commissioned by the railway tycoon Leland Stanford to produce photographic evidence that the entire body of a horse in movement was, at some point in its trajectory through space, unconnected to the earth. At Stanford's estate in Palo Alto, California, in 1878, Muybridge successfully created the first image-sequences of animal motion, using an arrangement of multiple cameras in order to photograph Stanford's horses, and thereby inventing the essential moving-image technology necessary for film itself to come into existence. He expanded his experiments from animal to human motion, and then devised a means to project his image-sequences to audiences, with his Zoopraxiscope machine demonstrating the results for scientific audiences in London and Paris in 1882, and for paying audiences in a pavilion at the Chicago World's Fair in 1893, two years before the Skladanowsky Brothers's film screening. Film's origin slips elusively back in time, and the impossibility of definitively pinpointing film's death is the result of the parallel impossibility of determining its exact origin; all of the motivations and ambitions that impelled the strange, non-collaborating group of in-fighting magicians, eccentric inventors, wallpaper designers, engineers and con-men who surround film's origins, and who conjured film into existence, are equally at work at the moment of film's death.

The spaces of cinema are the determining sites in which to observe the collision between film's origins and its end. When the first of the twelve cinemas of Los Angeles's Broadway was built in 1910, the American film industry had not yet been transplanted from New York and Chicago to Hollywood; by 1931, when the last Broadway cinema was constructed, 21 years later, the zenith of those cinemas had already passed, and the lavish constructions had now become death-inflected, their inbuilt process of glorious decay ready for activation. The spaces of cinema form a receptive arena for the transformative compacting-together of obsessional memories about film's origins and ends. In her book on Eadweard Muybridge, the cultural historian Rebecca Solnit, preoccupied above all with images of horses – and with interrogating how Muybridge created his image-sequences of horses in movement – conjures up a childhood memory of cinema-going that amalgamates an obsolescent kind of cinematic experience (of watching a generic Western) with the perceptual revelation of witnessing how filmic images are generated, and projected to the human eye:

> I remember sitting in the darkness of movie theatres, a space that to a child seemed almost religious: so many people gathered together hushed to share the same thing, something more vivid than anything but life and more dramatic than ordinary life. In those days it always seemed to be western movies: horses galloping across deserts and wagon trains circling up on prairies. Every so often I would look up to watch the beam of light through the darkness above instead of the story on the screen. The light flickered, broke into several beams that corresponded to the action on the screen, and made it clear that the movie wasn't only a story but a medium, a rolling stream of light in the darkness. Up above in the projection booth would have been a stream of celluloid rushing by at the rate of a foot a second, making one of those western movies a trail of photographs miles long. The river of light and shadow and the trail of film had an origin, a source in those galloping horses and western landscapes, and it came back to that place, though the place was transformed.[6]

The Afterlives of Film

Film was always defined by its vital movements, impacts, and gestures, even when those gestures became inflected by an intentional
violence or aberrance that intimated its incipient downfall, and film's
imageries were dynamically propelled through space to their screen
as an act of revelatory illumination, forming, as Rebecca Solnit
noted, a 'river of light', that carried both those imageries and also
the inseparable technologies of their projection. If film was always
a living entity, in itself and also for its audiences, what now happens
to film – and to the spaces conceived and constructed for film, often
with extreme extravagance and architectural excess, in cities worldwide – after its multiple deaths?

In one sense, film mutated, rather than died, and brokered its
future subsistence through accepting a minor role as a variant
enmeshed within the proliferating forms of the digital medium:
even shot, edited and projected digitally, as numerical data-pixels,
film could still expect to generate some of its previous impact and
sensation, either through the enduring momentum carried by the
act of engulfing into itself all culture, all history, all human vision,
for a period of a century or so, or else because it still employed the
same kind of narrative forms, even if they now often appeared to
have been urgently concertinaed, which it had used while still a distinctive medium in its own right. In that case, little of consequence
would have been changed by film's death, and the subsumed status
of its posthumous existence, even relegated to that of the walking
dead, would still recognisably be that of film. Similarly, the new
spaces of film mutated, but remained designated as cinemas. In cities
for which film had been a vital presence, such as Riga, birthplace
of Sergei Eisenstein on 23 January 1898, the grandiose cinemas in
the central avenues of the city became abandoned or destroyed in
the opening years of the twenty-first century, but a proliferation of

cinema-complexes, each identical, appeared instead in the vast hypermarkets built along the city's arterial highways, and in the basements of the multi-tiered corporate plazas on its peripheries, as though expelled from the city. Again, nothing would have been essentially changed by the death of cinema's spaces, if the voiding of its sensorial charge could still allow a vacuous black room, with a minuscule screen at one end for the projection of digital images, to be identified as constituting a cinema. But since film and its spaces had always defined themselves through their extraordinary capacity to transform, unsettle and overhaul human vision, such an act of identification would demand the complicity of eyes that had been voided as comprehensively as the posthumous forms of film and its spaces.

Film's post-death ghostworld also, and contrarily, involved an afterlife existence located in a parallel dimension, or at an irreconcilable tangent, to that banal subsistence within the acquisitive portfolio of digital media. An essential element of that afterlife is formed from the way in which film scarred its obsessive and luxuriant imagination into human cultures, setting off chain reactions of imagery, extending far beyond the ostensible domain of film, thereby embedding that imagination profoundly within the forms of art, and within a multiplicity of ways to approach and confront the experiences of life. Film's ghostworld is also a volatile terrain of memory, always present as a layer ingrained in human consciousness, and subject to moments of sudden, intensive resuscitation that parallel the way in which Sergei Eisenstein perceived the film-editing process, as the conjunction of often divergent images into new constellations, with the power to incite sensory activations within human memory, not to invoke lost sensations or images in a Proustian sense, but instead to generate an arms-cache of images for an active confrontation with the present moment. Film's posthumous existence has the form of an eruptive archive of memory.

Film's post-death spatial forms are also those of its abandoned cinemas, whether left to deteriorate into ruination in their own time, or else converted for re-use – as nightclubs, spaces of human habitation, cultist churches, markets, subterranean gymnasia, secret hideouts, or an infinity of other uses. Film's ghost-spaces are also those of cinemas worldwide that have been demolished and wiped out of existence – a strategy initiated almost as soon as cinemas' industries began, with the transition from nickelodeon venues to more fully formed cinema spaces, and again in the technological transition from the spaces of silent cinema to those of sound, among many other imperatives that rendered film's spaces redundant and consigned them to destruction. Every destroyed cinema space has a virtual counterpart in its survival through fragments of evidence, traces of memory, or simply through an ineradicable filmic aura. Film's posthumous spaces are also those with pre-determined usages which film infiltrated only temporarily, or even momentarily, such as the venues of the first film screenings for paying audiences, the Wintergarten Ballroom in Berlin and the Grand Café in Paris, in 1895, before the conception of a specific architecture for film had come into existence; even outdoor spaces, such as those inhabited by itinerant cinemas (consisting only of portable materials: a projector, a screen, and film reels), like that witnessed as a child by the French writer Jean Genet in the isolated village of Alligny-en-Morvan in the 1910s, could form seminally charged sites with a delayed creative explosivity, as for Genet's future work, long after those spatially improvised cinemas had moved on and vanished. The strange power of film's ghostworlds is especially apparent when they are abruptly reactivated, as with the unique screenings of Steve McQueen's film-works *Western Deep* and *Caribs' Leap*, staged as an installation within the core of the long-abandoned, gutted Lumière cinema in London, in October 2002, with the spectators seated on the raw concrete of the subterranean cinema's

infrastructure. Abandoned cinemas – whether left to disintegrate, obliviously re-used, conjured only from a momentary spatial
inhabitation, or else resuscitated into filmic life – constitute the
sensitized zones in which to explore film's end.

Cinema's Two Abandonments

What remains of cinema is abandoned: abandoned images, abandoned buildings, together with a volatile set of traces compacted
from memory, obsession, corporeality, imagination, excess, and
sensory responses and impacts. Because that detritus forms an
unruly amalgam, the dereliction of cinema has a contrary and split
form, which encompasses two abandonments: first, an abandonment which is directed at whatever has survived the multiple deaths
of cinema, especially the buildings in which film's audiences were
located for their experience; and second, an abandonment which
is integrally a human one, taking place when an annulling power
of restriction imposed on the senses or behaviour or memory has
been eluded, and an abandonment of that power results, in which
the body also wildly abandons and unleashes itself – in the context
of visual media, to experience new acts of vision. That self-
abandonment has resonances with Rimbaud's demands for a 'seer'
– literally someone whose mission is to see, to see through and
beyond – and who exacts that abandonment through a 'prodigious
and rational disordering of all the senses':[7] an act which requires
both the intentional ending of a previous sensory system, and also
the endurance, even in a state of terminal ruination, of an identifiable location, such as that of film, in which that disordering can
operate. Abandoned cinemas provide that location.

In their ruination, cinemas must still carry the markings of
their previous mission, in order for those two forms of abandonment to operate. The site of the screen must be discernible, even if

Rialto cinema marquee (fragment).

that screen has now been dismantled, ripped or hidden. The place of the audience should be traceable, though the tiers of seats may have vanished long ago. The projection-box needs to be locatable, even if it is now broken apart, with the projectors and film reels absent. And some trace of the cinema's exterior insignia within the surrounding context of the city – the neon lettering of its sign, the frames for its film-posters or hoardings, or the architectural form of its marquee – must be there for the eye to discover, even if, as with the cinemas of Los Angeles's Broadway, the marquees' exclamations of film have often become overlayered with advertisements for clothing or plasma televisions. An intention to leave those structures behind, to render them obsolete, or simply to consign them to oblivion – an intention to erase memory – needs to be ingrained in their current appearance. Abandonment constitutes an active recognition that a presence with a distinctive or extraordinary visual identity had once existed, but that that presence, at some moment in the past or in the contemporary moment, is one requiring supplantation, eradication, either as part of the ongoing scrambling for pre-eminent visibility of a city's elements, or through a contemptuous dismissal of what had once made that presence extraordinary. But that act, in leaving its spurned object stranded in an interzone, in limbo, not entirely erased, still with a hair's breadth chance of resuscitation, may also form a loving abandonment.

The sensory abandonment presented by the ruination of cinematic space is one generated precisely by that disorientatingly knife-edged positioning between disappearance and resurgence, between a cruel and loving effacement. Rather than heading further into a complete cancellation of visuality, the ruination of film's site appears also to offer itself an alternative direction, guided out of darkness (as though by an oracle or Rimbaudian 'seer') by the essential aberrance and volatility of the filmic medium itself throughout its history, as one uniquely sensitized for imaginative,

In Search of a Midnight Kiss, 2008.

and often for revolutionary, liberation. Film will not go quietly. The interzonal site of abandonment – neither intact, nor ruined beyond recognition – is one in critical flux, whose instability has the ability to engender sensations that look forward towards the creation of new visual formations and unforeseen experiences. That position of limbo is also one in which the resonances of film's imageries have been subordinated to those of digital culture, but in which the supplanting imageries possess a profound insufficiency of vision in relation to those generated by film, and appear to operate within narrow corporate parameters that are not at the level of the human eye's demands. The imperative, then, would be to envisage a set of future imageries that emerged directly from the multiple deaths of cinema, and out of the memory-ingrained, strange spaces of film's abandonment, which might have a liberatory and unrestricted scope of expansion. In that disordering, the negation attached to film's abandonment would have its counterpart in an unleashing of the eye.

The experience of those two contrary but conjoined forms of abandonment is made explicit in the 2008 film *In Search of a Midnight Kiss*, in which a young couple, Vivian and Wilson, who have just met, are wandering through Los Angeles on New Year's Eve, and happen on the derelict cinemas of Broadway. Vivian observes that the cinemas have become the 'lockers' of the city, hidden spaces with unknown contents, and wants to go inside one of them. Wilson persuades a security guard to allow them momentary access to the interior of one of the cinemas (they are outside the Orpheum cinema, but through one of the outlandish displacements integral to film, the interior space they enter is actually that of the Million Dollar Theater, at the far end of Broadway). Vivian and Wilson experience their entry into the vast, ornate interior of the abandoned cinema as an ecstatic transition into excessive sensory and imaginative release, as they immediately begin to fantasize, in a vocabulary of calamitous events and sexual actions determined by film's memory and film's narratives, about what they would do or create if that space of abandonment was placed under their power, as it now is, if only transiently. Having entered the cinema at balcony level, close to its cracked but intricately decorated cranial roof, they are impelled towards the location of the screen, and descend to stand on the stage in a bright light, like that of a projector-beam, in front of the source of the cinema's images, for its now-void audience. But the film screen, as the core of that deteriorated building, has disappeared, and the couple's wild sensory disordering, precipitated intensively but momentarily by their entry into that interzonal space, has a rational element: Wilson notes that the abandoned cinema 'is dead'. Without that aura of death, there could be no extravagant imaginative release.

Film's Hauntings

If an abandoned cinema is dead, as the characters of In Search of a Midnight Kiss conclude, that state of death is a strangely living one, able to precipitate abundant fantasies (darkly filmic fantasies, of sex and of death itself) and obsessions, and to vivify the sensation of ecstatic bewilderment, experienced and exclaimed by Wilson and Vivian, that emerges from the traversal of the boundary that separates the living city from the haunted space of the derelict cinema. One factor in that sensorially charged traversal may be that the city which is left behind – with its homogeneous corporate imperatives and its digitized environment – is even less alive than the abandoned cinema into which its necrophiliac explorers cross over. The impact of haunting carried by the disintegrated or re-used spaces of cinema results from a simultaneity of vision in which the entire temporal history of a cinema, with its contrary phases of glory and destitution, is compressed into the present moment, since the integrity of its filmic history has disintegrated along with its architectural infrastructure (the history of cinema's spaces is one of the great black holes in the historical documentation of film, and when a cinema becomes abandoned, and its records discarded, that neglect is exacerbated still more), with the result that any moment in a cinema's existence can abruptly resurge at will into the present, like a ghost-presence in a horror film, sonically underscored by the

In Search of a Midnight Kiss, 2008.

cacophony of memory. In that oblivious levelling of a cinema's history, each of its distinctive phases becomes equivalent to every other, and its temporal hierarchy is erased: the moment at which it served as a riotous all-night site for cult-film mania or pornography becomes inseparable from that of its prestigious moment of ascendancy as the venue for searchlight-illuminated star-premieres. Time blurs, stops dead, and transmits itself intensively and multiply in the abandoned cinema, like a celluloid film-image trapped in the projector-gate, heated to incandescence before it finally burns up and vanishes.

In ghost films, the haunting of space is perceived in fragments. Space becomes excessive and horrifying since it cannot be seen in its entirety; it dissolves to the point at which its elements cannot be clearly identified because the film's character is hallucinating with fear, or is now too terrified to recognize the habitual parameters of life. To resolve that extreme disorientation, the human eye is required to do extraordinary work, to pivot backwards in order to look behind the haunted body, or stretch to see into darkness, hidden space, and into the zones of peripheral vision – but all that can be unearthed is yet more evidence of death or haunting: new terrors. The space of the abandoned cinema carries that ocular challenge in an acute form, especially when the cinema has entered

Filmic hauntings – Rialto cinema interior.

a condition of almost terminal ruination in which the reassembly of its space within human vision appears initially insoluble, and in that vulnerable condition of disorientation, in which filmic space cannot be mapped, its multiple and past lives appear at their most tangible. The hauntedness of abandoned cinemas is enhanced by the fact that cinemas were often the preferred site for murders, violent assaults and suicides, either as a result of the cut-throat competitiveness of film's early exhibitors of the 1910s and '20s, or because the engulfing experience of film may intensify sensations to breaking point, and its spaces annul the boundary between what can and cannot be undertaken (a cinematic exemption from reality which fascinated the Surrealist filmmakers, notably Buñuel and Artaud, among other artists preoccupied not only with film, but with the spaces of film), with implications for acts entailing both death and sex, so that abandoned cinemas are perpetually haunted by the residues of sexual passions as well as by their auras of death.

Once film has experienced its multiple deaths, and its spaces have become irreparably abandoned, the human eye takes on an enhanced status and becomes pivotal in the impossible process of assembling filmic detritus into a recognizable form, as well as assuming the mission – a mission that had pre-eminently been film's, for a period of a century or more – to instigate and project new forms of vision. But the eye has to proceed carefully, like that of a character exploring a disintegrating and ghostly space in a horror film: with every step, the floorboards may give way, leading to a limitless plummeting into darkness, or the ghost-presences excessively surrounding film may envelop the eye completely. The fragments of vision caught by the wildly searching eye in a horror film have to accumulate, to form a way forwards, towards a terminal point of exit. But in the haunted space of the abandoned cinema, film's end is only the beginning of the eye's work.

The Fall into Abandonment

If film is at its end, that blackout involves a fall that spins consciousness, memory and the senses together into a delirious plummeting, and which oscillates between the preoccupations of film narrative itself and the terminal moments of the history of film and of its unique spaces. A fall in film is often exhilarating and ecstatic, entailing the wilful sensory self-abandonments induced by film, but those sensations are intimately close to those of terror-inflected negation and vanishing, to an unwilled overturning of the human body. Film involves a movement into darkness, both in terms of its offering of an initiation into unknown terrains that always captivated and enthralled its audiences, from the first moments of film history when film's imageries propelled its spectators into strange new landscapes, and also through the audience's entry into an enticing architectural space which, though initially illuminated to display its extravagant design and attributes as the prelude to the main spectacle, was then abruptly plunged into darkness, with the audience hushing itself into silence in order to reinforce its own receptivity to whatever images materialized to pierce that darkness.

Mulholland Drive,
2001.

Mulholland Drive,
2001.

With the abandonment of cinema's spaces, that fall into the dark becomes explicit, and its aspects of negation and vanishing appear uppermost; in California, on the ticket-kiosk of Santa Barbara's most spectacular cinema, designed in an ornate Spanish Mission architectural style in 1931, complete with a long courtyard and fountains, and now disused, a sign announces: 'Arlington Cinema: Dark'. That fall into the abandoned cinema's darkness precipitates a powerful engulfing of the senses, with a distinctive corporeal and visual impact.

In David Lynch's 2001 film *Mulholland Drive*, that plummeting into darkness is sited explicitly in abandoned cinematic space, within the transformative terrain of the disused cinemas of Los Angeles's Broadway. Lynch's film also demonstrates an experience of a centrifugal urban geography of Los Angeles that has resulted from film's cancellation; since film has perversely disappeared from the seminal film-city, the eye moves instead to the surface of the city itself and constructs trajectories across its raw, skinned-alive parameters, in order to locate any surviving evidence of film and of its vital ruination. The film's two lovers, Betty and Rita, meet after Rita, who is being driven to a dark, peripheral site in order to be murdered there, becomes the sole survivor of a head-on car collision on Mulholland Drive – a winding, unlit road (named after William Mulholland, the notorious water engineer who worked above the Million Dollar Theater) that follows the crest of the Hollywood Hills. Rita's memory is erased by the accident's trauma, and she descends the precipitous hillside into Hollywood's avenues, where she infiltrates herself into Betty's apartment. After she and Betty make love, Rita repeatedly cries out the word 'silencio' in her sleep, at two in the morning, and insists that Betty 'go with me somewhere'. They make a journey by taxi across Los Angeles, from Hollywood to Downtown, initially encountering that district's corporate banking towers, before penetrating further, into the darkness and wind-blown dereliction of Broadway, to reach the Club Silencio, located in an abandoned cinema, the Tower. Like Vivian and Wilson in *In Search of a Midnight Kiss*, Betty and Rita are irresistibly drawn inside

Tower cinema facade.

the cinema's space, but for a far darker experience of sensory abandonment than those other lovers.

The entry into the cinema's interior propels Betty and Rita into an engulfing and awry zone, marked by the disparity between the minuscule exterior doorway of the Club Silencio, with its ramshackle neon sign facing a bleak car-park, and the grandiose interior of the Tower cinema, with its red velvet curtaining, intricately carved terracotta balconies and disintegrating domed roof. The Tower cinema was constructed in 1927 in an amalgam of Moorish and Baroque styles by the young cinema architect S. Charles Lee, who would also design the far larger Los Angeles Theater, further north on Broadway; Lee aimed to generate future commissions through his designs for the Tower, intending both its interior and exterior as demonstrations of extreme extravagance. Although the Tower was one of the first of Los Angeles's sound-equipped cinemas, at the moment of transition from silent to sound cinema, and went on to become a blaring, permanently open newsreel cinema during the 1940s war years, *Mulholland Drive* propels that space backwards, into silence, as the Club Silencio. Betty and Rita enter the cinema's balcony area, where a scattering of mute spectators are awaiting the performance.

The Tower cinema is not showing a film: the screen is gone, replaced by a microphone and lavish curtains. But the space's aura of engulfing cinematic abandonment survives its mutation into the Club Silencio, and determines the corporeal response of Betty and Rita to the spectacle. The sinister master of ceremonies announces that everything to be seen and heard in that space is an illusion; Betty convulses in her seat as the master of ceremonies stares upwards at her, before he conjures himself away into smoke-screened disappearance. The singer Rebekah del Rio then appears in dishevelled make-up, like an actress from a film melodrama of

Mulholland Drive,
2001.

wild emotions, and, unaccompanied, performs a Spanish-language version of Roy Orbison's song *Crying*. Betty and Rita appear lost, deeply drawn into the spectacle, physically and sensorially immersed to the point of extreme disorientation. A shot of the cinema's balcony area, illuminated in blue light, reveals that the two lovers' derangement is far in excess of that of the remainder of the sparse audience, with Rita gripping Betty's shoulders, both women deliriously pinioned into their experience. Then, Rebekah del Rio suddenly loses consciousness in mid-song, and collapses to the ground to end her performance, though the sound of her singing persists after her fall. Betty's attention is immediately drawn to her purse, in which an unfamiliar box has materialized, and whose investigation, after the two lovers abruptly leave the cinema, will cause them both to vanish without trace, consigning them, on their dreamer's awakening, to figures of obsession in a dark dream about film.

When film's figures (its momentary lovers, in *Mulholland Drive* and *In Search of a Midnight Kiss*) enter the space of abandoned cinemas – spaces left to disintegrate, as in the Million Dollar Theater, or else transformed, as into a hallucinatory nightclub, in the Tower cinema – they are immersed into a precarious, contrary terrain in which the residual aura of film's aberrant imageries, and its industries' often sinister history, has been intensified by the process of abandonment, and causes those figures to be engulfed by a power which far exceeds their habitual sensory capacities. In that darkened space, an unprecedented experience of film's cancelled power irresistibly seizes those loving intruders, but that experience will always end in a sensory or corporeal fall, into an intimacy with darkness or death.

Film's Destructivity

Film is a perverse medium that (unlike photographic or digital media) has always wilfully used itself to castigate its own industries and forms, to denounce its own dreams, to disintegrate and fragment its own imageries and narratives; even the nostalgia for film is powered by an attraction for film's integral destructivity, which is equally tangible, in American cinema, across both art film and mainstream Hollywood film. Lynch's work compacts those two strands of film, art film and mainstream film, into a volatile amalgam, thereby deepening the impact and exacerbating the darkness and destructivity of each strand, whenever that work, as in *Mulholland Drive*, focuses upon film and the film industry itself. *Mulholland Drive* envisions a mysterious Hollywood film industry in which an interconnected cabal of impenetrable figures (such as The Cowboy, who inhabits a corral underneath the Hollywood Sign, where he chides recalcitrant film directors and instructs them in their casting imperatives) are able to determine the celebrity and deaths of figures such as Rita and Betty, who are film actresses, albeit amnesiac or desperate ones. Since the earliest years of American cinema, an industry of scandal documentation and the systematic probing of film's celebrities has doubled the film industry. Notably, the experimental filmmaker Kenneth Anger's legendary book *Hollywood Babylon* (1959) draws on that unstable intersection between art film and mainstream film in order to position its archiving of the multiple depravities, jealousies and killings that corrode American cinema's history, within a textual form that accords Hollywood's fragile celebrities the same kind of malign, doomed glamour that Anger also imparts to the figures in his experimental films, such as New York's leatherclad bikers in *Scorpio Rising* (1964), or the Hitler Youth pioneers in *Ich Will!* (2008). Film appears to have originated with a compulsion to annul its own glories, and simultaneously to create a lavish documentation of that process of erasure.

Innumerable films have anatomized the American film industry's location in Los Angeles, and pinpointed an unparalleled axis for the dissolution of human identity within that urban environment. The titles of Los Angeles-situated films, such as Wilder's *Sunset Boulevard* (1950), Polanski's *Chinatown* (1974), and Lynch's *Mulholland Drive* and *Inland Empire* (2006), indicate the symbiotic intimacy between film and Los Angeles itself, as both the originating site for the glorious expansion of the American cinema industry, and the urban entity that, once conjured into existence as an opaque megalopolis through the medium of film (and through the wide-scale corruption associated with William Mulholland's projects), negatively acted back upon the power that had created it, instilling destruction into film, which itself possessed its own dynamics of self-willed implosion, encompassing everything it came into contact with. In that scenario of film's destructivity, the abandonment of Los Angeles's cinemas, pre-eminently those of the Broadway area of Downtown, would result both from the need to eradicate the destabilizing presence of film from the city, in its most distinctively visible urban forms (replacing it with anonymous, homogeneous multiplex cinemas, buried deep in malls and retail parks), but also, contrarily, from the need to preserve the ruination of those spaces, so that the moment of the end of film could be maintained indefinitely in an almost cryogenic form, since without the survival of any defining, vivifying trace of film, the now digitized city of Los Angeles would cease to exist.

Film's destructivity, with its impact exerted on human identity and on its own industry, has a counterpart in the destruction of film's materials themselves: the celluloid and other media associated, throughout film's history until the onset of digital technologies, with the registration and projection of filmic images. In the early decades of film, its materials were regarded as having no value once a film was perceived to have yielded the total income that could be

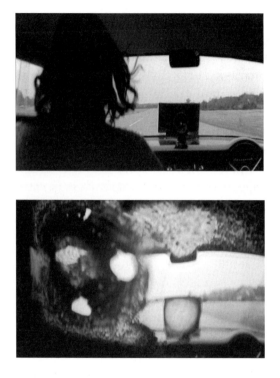

Two-Lane Blacktop,
1971.

generated from it through a finite number of screenings; although
no new set of images could be imprinted into film celluloid in order
to re-use it, its materials could be sifted for the exploitation of its
component chemical elements. The vast body of 'lost' films that is
essential to filmic history has a source in the systematic destruction
or discarding of its irreplaceable materials. Especially in the 1960s
and '70s, experimental filmmakers working in the USA, Japan and
Europe became preoccupied with the implications of actively
destroying their own film works (either to accentuate the memory
of the lost film, or else to experience the elation of the process of
destruction), and also with creating imageries of film's destruction.
Some of those preoccupations with the wilful disintegration of film

– together with its resonances for human identity, and for the power of film industries to infinitely replicate film's imageries – entered the idiosyncratic filmmaking that was especially prominent in Hollywood in that era, as in Monte Hellman's film about obsessive American race-journeys, *Two-Lane Blacktop* (1971), where the film ends (and film itself ends), as the celluloid images of the character called The Driver are abruptly halted, becoming one final and unique image, which burns and dissolves. The tenacious survival of film and its distinctive spaces, together with film's persistent significance within the digital era, appear to exist as an essential counterpoint to its long, intricate history of self-destructivity, and to its preoccupation with dreams of its own erasure.

Last Acts of Vision

The film image of burning celluloid, presented to the original cinema spectators of *Two-Lane Blacktop* as both the last image of the film whose America-wide car-race narrative they had followed, and also as film's own self-incendiary image, indicates the extraordinary power of terminal visual events, and of last screenings. Cinema's abandonment originates at the moment when a proprietor or distributor determines that a particular cinematic space has become moribund (often, as in the case of the cinemas of Los Angeles's Broadway, after increasingly desperate and abrupt switches in cinematic content, from mainstream films to specialist, cult or martial arts films, and finally to pornography), and that space must now be abandoned to ruination in perpetuity, or transformed through its re-use. Last screenings form seminal events, at which the ever-dwindling audience of a cinema is momentarily reversed, and a capacity audience often materializes to witness that last screening, whose impact is accentuated by the certainty that there will be nothing beyond it: a void or abyss, without images, through which the human eye cannot guide itself coherently, so that the terminal spectators, as a final act of vision, must intensively absorb the images at stake before cinema's precipice of darkness. American cinema reflected on the sensorial and corporeal implications of such moments in Peter Bogdanovich's film *The Last Picture Show*, on the events surrounding the closure of an already ramshackle cinema, made in that same year of prescient unease about film's future, 1971, as *Two-Lane Blacktop* and Dennis Hopper's drug-infused meditation on the disintegration of human vision and of the filmmaking process itself, *The Last Movie*. More recently, the Taiwanese filmmaker Tsai Ming-Liang's *Goodbye, Dragon Inn* (2003) is located entirely within the space of a grandiose but now-decrepit Taipei film-palace on the very last night of its operation.

A counterpart to the space of abandoned cinemas exists in the storage spaces or archives for films which can no longer be projected, since the technology of film-projection has shifted to that of digital media. For the proprietors of the innumerable rooms of obsolete celluloid film-reels that constellate the peripheries of Los Angeles's film studios and distribution companies, and similar haunted spaces worldwide, the imperative is that also faced by the 1920s proprietors of films deemed to have exhausted their earnings potential, and which were manually hacked apart with axes to facilitate the recycling of their raw materials. Film must be destroyed, or else becomes a detritus that accumulates in infinite quantities. Even the archives of national film museums possess an aura of obsolescence that results from the sudden blur in time, around the centenary of film, that rendered those archives' precious resources void, since the digital projection of the same film content will infinitely enhance its visual textures, avoid its transportation, and elude the breakdowns and deteriorations that always plagued celluloid projection. Occasionally, the spaces of cinemas and film archives collide in their final moments: a near-moribund cinema in Naples, the Casanova, has a foyer crammed to the roof with film-cans containing reels that had become stranded in space, no longer projectable and no longer worth returning to their distributor, thereby allowing them to form a vital terminal moraine of film's end, and an archival filmic spectacle in their own right.

The end of film is inflected by the obsession among its nostalgic advocates that its materials merit saving, and need to be systematically preserved within a cryogenic state (like that of those abandoned cinemas which, through accident or design, remain indefinitely frozen in their moment of ruination), in the expectation that, at some future moment, through a time-twisting aberration in the forms of visual media or an engulfing digital crash that will render the digital medium inoperable, film's moment will return. In that case, the death of film could be overruled, and its materials posthumously resuscitated, even in an impaired state, as in a zombie cult film. Equally, though, the opposite process, of an accelerated and capricious obliteration of all traces of film, of its surviving materials and its enduring cinematic spaces, could reactivate film by imparting a unique intensity to its destruction, and allowing the terminal spectators of that process to experience an all-consuming and momentary intimacy with film, with all of its sensory and mythic power, as it flares for the last time.

In the late 1980s the German artist Anselm Kiefer, preoccupied with the myths of the human species at extreme points in its existence, created a steel assemblage containing film-reels made of lead, with accompanying film cameras made from the same materials, and trailing fragments of leaden celluloid, as an annex to his monumental construction of an archive of lead books, *Zweistromland/ The High Priestess*, exhibiting them together at his retrospective exhibition at the Neue Nationalgalerie in Berlin in 1991. Kiefer's conjoining of the book and the film indicates that they possess an allied, revelatory power, but must now be perceived in that uniquely ineradicable state (their medium of lead able to survive a nuclear event or other act of attempted erasure), in which the content of text and image cannot be read or seen, and only the mythic spectacle of the archive itself persists, as mysterious knowledge. Kiefer's work projects the entity of film into a state beyond its own survival, transmutated into a now-petrified form that still induces an intensive act of spectatorship from its viewer, but from which all of the history of film, and all of film's imageries, have seeped out, like a radioactive detritus. A last act of vision, as with that of Kiefer's work, and of archival forms and terminal cinematic events, demands acute work from the human eye.

Film's Extreme Environments

Abandoned cinemas form landscapes of disintegration, with the interior ground levels of many cinemas, derelict and gutted for numerous years, as with the Rialto cinema in Los Angeles's Broadway, resembling the zero-terrains of accumulated debris and scorched-earth erasure that prominently appear in Anselm Kiefer's paintings of Europe's voided, scarred landscapes. The cinemas' untended walls and ceilings crack; botched attempts to convert them for re-use leave behind the discarded detritus of those curtailed projects; intruders contribute innumerable alcohol containers, syringes and crack-pipes to the amassing of a terminal landscape; the bodies of birds, that have entered through broken windows or fire-doors, and become trapped, constellate the ground, along with those of various species of rodents; and vast quantities of earth, plaster, broken glass and finely ground brick and stone, all of unknown provenance and mysterious purpose, materialize in the auditoria of abandoned cinemas, so that negotiating trajectories through those spaces becomes a precarious corporeal manoeuvre. Those interior cinematic landscapes constitute film's extreme environments – incorporating film's end, together with that of human vision – and possess their intimate counterparts in corresponding exterior landscapes which have fascinated filmmakers, pre-eminent among them that of the desert panoramas of Death Valley, on the eastern periphery of California, where Michelangelo Antonioni shot the pivotal scenes for his film *Zabriskie Point* in 1970.

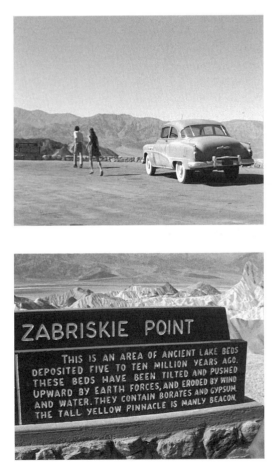

Zabriskie Point, 1970.

Even before Antonioni travelled to Death Valley, its landscape of human erasure – the hottest point on the planet, and infinitely hostile to the human species – had perversely intersected with film. In the mid-1910s, a railway was built into the valley, and during the 1920s Hollywood film crews began to use it as a distinctive location for Westerns, with that extravagantly barren desert-landscape prefiguring the subsequent adoption of Monument Valley, further to the east in Arizona, as the Western's emblematic landscape. Death Valley possessed a cinema, at the railway's terminus in the mining town of Ryan, perched on the mountainside surrounding the valley, and spectators gathered for weekly screenings in the ramshackle wooden building. But by 1930 the railway had closed down; soon, the town of Ryan was abandoned by its inhabitants and then razed by its environment, so that not only had all trace of the cinema disappeared, but the town itself had fallen through the map, leaving no tangible evidence of its existence.[8] Film re-manifested itself in Death Valley only after 40 years, with the arrival of Antonioni's film crew on the nearby promontory of Zabriskie Point. As with the interior space of abandoned cinemas, the extreme environment of Death Valley intensified human vision to an unstable condition, on a boundary between ocular survival and negation. And as *Zabriskie Point* demonstrates, that environment also delineates a unique interzone where the eye pivots between a delirious exhilaration (a specifically sexual exhilaration, for Antonioni) integral to its intimacy with abandonment's aura – taking the form of a wildly excessive unleashing of the eye – and an experience of erasure which leaves behind at most an afterburn trace or blur, and no memory.

The two young lovers Mark and Daria arrive at Zabriskie Point having only just met; Mark has fled a lethal student riot in Los Angeles, stealing a light plane and, after flying low over Daria's car, landing it in the remote Californian desert, where Daria encounters him by chance. They then travel together to Death Valley by car and

speed up the sliproad to the Zabriskie Point look-out. That landscape is one of supreme desolation and maximal emptiness (no
other human figures can be seen), in excess of all other deserts'
powers, but also strangely corporeal in form, and lividly coloured
by mineral deposits. Daria and Mark leave the car and sit on the
wall enclosing the look-out point, transfixed by the landscape, as
though they were watching a film. Although that experience is a
captivating one, it is also one that mediates death – like Wilson at
the Million Dollar Theater in *In Search of a Midnight Kiss*, Mark
remarks that what he sees 'is dead'. That landscape is one of human
abandonment – beyond the human, and left behind by the miners
and entrepreneurs who had attempted to exploit it – but also one
that precipitates sensory abandonment, in an oscillation between
the vulnerable eye and the vivifying filmic landscape that entails a
sonic dimension; as Matthew Gandy notes: 'The bleached landscape appears to listen and respond to the human figures, creating
its own echo of spatial intimation.'[9] That sensory abandonment
entails both the abrupt descent by Daria and Mark into the landscape, to make love on the desert floor, within its corporeal
formations, and also Daria's ecstatic hallucination that not only she
and Mark are making love, but the entire landscape of Zabriskie
Point is orgiastically saturated with sexually engaged figures. The
explicitly filmic experience which Daria and Mark have undergone
is underlined by the intruder who appears just as they leave the
landscape – the oblivious driver of a mobile home, who gapes at
the landscape and exclaims: 'They should build a drive-in up here.
They'd make a mint.' But the erasure-landscape of Death Valley,
like the ruination of cinemas, cancels out its exploitation.

As with *Two-Lane Blacktop*, the narrative of Antonioni's film ends
with an imagery of film's own end, in the all-consuming detonation
which Daria's imagination unleashes, after she hears on her car-
radio that Mark, who has left her behind to fly back to Los Angeles,

Zabriskie Point, 1970.

has been killed by the police on landing. It is Daria's physical abandonment, in her now-terminal separation from her momentary
lover, that precipitates the unrestrained, explosive fury of her
imagination, against the power that has brought about her abandonment. That detonation is one focused on a cliffside house that
embodies America's power of corruption and its consumer culture.
Since cinema itself cannot self-detonate in that space – film is

operating as the explosive instrument exerting the impact of Daria's imagination – film's disposable visual-media counterpart is instead that of the television set that spectacularly fragments as Daria's imagination blows it apart. The resulting aerial landscape of velocity-impelled shards itself forms an extreme environment, like that of Death Valley's corporeal, filmic forms or the accumulated debris-layers within the space of abandoned cinemas. Film ends in an infinity of imageries of its own disintegration. Antonioni, who had not enjoyed his experience of collaboration with the Hollywood studios, had originally intended to end his film by having a sky-writing plane inscribe the words 'Fuck You, America!' in letters of smoke in the skies over Los Angeles, but was prevented from doing so. Whenever a film announces 'The End' at its closure – as *Zabriskie Point* does, when Daria turns her back on her own vision of destruction, and vanishes into nightfall – it has telescoped its entire narrative up until that point into one scene, or one moment, of special significance, elucidation or impact, in order to reach a culmination that takes place immediately before that textual signalling of its closure: a forcible abandonment, even a destruction, of the experience of the film, for its spectator's eye, which may well want to see more, to go further and deeper. But 'The End' freezes the eye.

Pioneers of Film's End

Film's pioneers, at the origins of cinema, were those impelled to go further and deeper (like the topographical pioneers of several decades earlier, who had first entered the unliveable environment of Death Valley in their perilous attempts to reach the Californian coast), and to explore the areas beyond the spatial, temporal and technological limitations of then current media, such as still photography and slide projection. Those pioneers – such as Eadweard Muybridge, Louis Le Prince, Wordsworth Donisthorpe, William

Dickson, the Skladanowsky Brothers and the Lumière Brothers –
often worked in isolation and in hostility towards one another,
with contrary aims, allied only in their collective preoccupation
with the origins of a new form, which drew on previous media but
possessed a distinctive autonomy and velocity of its own that
(beyond their grasp) would gather momentum to become that of
film. Filmmakers or film artists working in the contemporary
moment operate within an exactly contrary set of parameters:
instead of expansively exploring the origination of film, they are
pioneers of film's end, of an apparent spatial closing down directed
towards film's terminal point, since abandonment implies a
boundaried constriction within which deterioration sets in. At the
same time, pioneering film's abandonment forms a profoundly
exploratory process that, powered by the aberrant visions of film in
its volatile state of decay, may unleash an unprecedented visual
form, and instigate new ways of configuring and envisioning the
human eye, since the homogeneous and corporatized forms associated with the onset of digital media are not fixed as the next step
following film.

The work of film's pioneers from the early 1870s to the mid-
1890s appears not to have been conceived as the instigation of a
vast, global industry that would determine the entirety of human
culture and imagination for the next century. In most cases, those
pioneers possessed individually motivated, ephemeral aims, with
wildly disparate forms: Muybridge investigated motion as a means
to take forward his previous work in photographing landscape-
panoramas; Donisthorpe devised a visual form that, if viewed by an
audience, could expand the impact of his libertarian political ideas.
In some cases, as with the Skladanowsky Brothers, whose involvement with the medium of film was intensive but short-lived, the
intention appears to have been to promote film as one particular,
magical variant among the other spectacles they were involved in

conjuring up. Other pioneers, with skills in engineering, became preoccupied, often to the point of obsession, with the painstaking analysis of technological obstacles, whose resolution marked the end of their involvement with film, since they were preoccupied in directly inverse proportion with the promotional and financial aspects of film. Many pioneers were convinced of the almost immediate redundancy of the work they were engaged in, or became subject to the caprices and overruling priorities of the magnates who commissioned their work and often arbitrarily cancelled it in mid-invention. Film's early pioneers appear always oblivious to the enormity of what they were unleashing, undertaking a sequence of uncertain and precarious gestures around the origination of an exploratory form that seemed often to resist its own coalescing and stratification into a medium.

By contrast, at the opposite extreme of film's existence, contemporary filmmakers and film artists operate with a determining awareness of the enormity of the medium they are working with, but simultaneously with an awareness of the foreclosed future of that medium, so that it is no longer unknown, but exhaustively known, to the point that the over-constrictive excess of that knowing of film may have petrified it, killed it. If something no longer possesses unknown zones, it cannot form the focus of the exploratory desires that would sustain it. And if film is dead, its temporal dimension has ended, so that pioneers of film's abandonment concentrate pre-eminently on investigating the spatial dimensions of film's disintegration, the ghostly and impenetrable spatial interzone between film's demise and the domain of the digital, the endangered human bodies that inhabit film's terminal spaces – and which, in contemporary filmmaking, such as the work of Wong Kar-Wai and David Lynch, often take the form of the blurred, irresoluble figures that were also prevalent at film's first, tentative moments, such as those captured in Louis Le Prince's films of the late 1880s. Alongside those filmic explorations that pioneer film's end, and which probe how its imageries can be manipulated or reinvented in film's last moments – as survival-areas for its human figures – it is also the spaces of cinematic abandonment that form seminal presences for charting the terminal outcome of film, since film's infinite spatial mutations may entail perverse, last-minute resuscitations as well as disappearances, even if those momentarily revivified spaces remain imbued with cinematic erasure.

Cinema's Die-Hards

Any manifestation of the survival of film, beyond its end, entails a spectacular instance of the persistence of vision: the principle by which the eye allows itself to believe that the interval separating two images is not inhabited by a void between two still, fixed images, but by a zone of movement created by the first image as it vanishes, and consolidated by the second, so that the vision of film remains in flux, and the carrying through of acts is perceived. Whether filmic persistence of vision really exists at all has been disputed for almost as long as film itself has existed; numerous other formulations of the mysterious or unknowable relationship between the film image and the human eye have been devised, and persistence of vision is itself a mythic conception of a mythic form. Even so, despite its fraudulence, the persistence of vision principle intimates the moment and space beyond film's death, in which vision permits its own beguiling, and thereby exposes itself, within that fragile time and that indeterminate domain, in order to experience the momentum of an intensive sensorial charge that has already evanesced. Once film itself has ended, its imageries may still be projected, as terminal events performed against the grain of the contemporary moment's technologies, and that sensorial charge of film then becomes one imbued with disintegration and obsolescence, in which human vision needs to participate still more profoundly, in the maintenance of the illusion of film's survival, entailing a self-willed abandonment that propels the eye into that deliquescing interzone of time and space.

Close to the birthplace of Sergei Eisenstein, at the grandiose but near-abandoned Kino Riga cinema – built in 1923 as the 'Splendid Palace' cinema during the same era of expansive construction as the cinemas of Los Angeles's Broadway, and later renamed after its city – the decision about whether to actually project the film at its advertised time, or to leave the auditorium empty for that film's duration, pivoted on a numerical knife-edge. As I waited to enter the cinema, the manager announced to the cashier and usherettes that the projection could go ahead only 'if three people come'. A strange interval ensued, like that of the persistence of vision, in which one spectator had arrived, but at least two more were required in order to fire the film's images into movement, and the entire staff focused their attention on the oblivious human figures outside the cinema, moving along the Elizabetes avenue. High above the cinema's foyer, the projectionist, too, was on hold, suspended. The set time for the screening passed. Then, two or three spectators nonchalantly materialized, as though unaware of their seminal role in the bringing into existence of film. Inside the extravagant auditorium, designed in an oval shape, and decorated in the form of a Rococo palace, with the chandeliers now cracked and the ornate golden palm trees along the nicotine-cream walls distressed, the manager announced to the scattered spectators that there would be a further delay, of fifteen minutes or so, since the projector had malfunctioned. The spectators dispersed to the lavish salon that served as the cinema's waiting room, and sprawled in the ancient green armchairs, as though exchanging one state of petrified corporeal stasis for another. Below the main auditorium, down a marble staircase, a fully abandoned smaller cinema, almost identical in its miniaturized form and with a similarly sumptuous, derelict salon of empty armchairs, was kept in near darkness, with a single lightbulb in the dead centre of the cherub-painted ceiling still illuminated. While the cinema above was half-heartedly heated, this space was frozen, its time lapsed. After half an hour, the spectators began to re-enter the main auditorium, the lights went down, and the projector overhead audibly ground itself into tenuous movement. The auditorium remained dark, and the spectators began to curse. It appeared to require an immense, collective effort of persistent will, as though generated from the infinitely accumulated capacities of visual and sensory fascination amassed throughout film's history, from those final die-hard participants of film's spectacle, even to envision the first image. Then the curtains opened, the screen appeared, and the film began.

After film's end, the industry of film gives the illusion of continuation, as though nothing had happened, and the momentary interval between film's disappearance and the pre-eminence of the digital image formed a natural event that is as immediately engrained within vision as the mythic illusions and aberrant neural transmissions that allowed the human eye to conjure film into movement. Media-industry corporations depend upon the invisibility of their own transformations and convulsions, and on the elision of a fundamental shift in the nature of the visual image – though that elision is often articulated in the familiar vocabulary and cadences of film, since film was always the medium that could effortlessly convince its audiences of the existence of the impossible, or coax a belief in illusions. Nothing possesses more power to beguile and entrance than a media conglomerate, and the endurance of such captivations in itself forms a legacy of film, even when that power becomes exercised for the corporate nullification of vision. In that sense, film's abandoned or last-ditch spaces, such as that of the

Kino Riga cinema or the ruined cinemas of Los Angeles's Broadway, appear to belong to a parallel universe from contemporary media industries, since they offer no clear destination-point for the eye that has entered the persistence of vision interval beyond film's final image, but is still awaiting the next image, that might give that interval its definition. The eye becomes uniquely stranded within the space of those abandoned cinemas, without the illusion of linear movement, and so needs to determine its own direction, deploying an intensive, exploratory resolution. Film's dereliction delineates an open space, of salutary disorientation, to conceive new visual forms.

First Cinemas' Ends

Once a cinema is abandoned, its natural inclination may be to enter a state of ongoing deterioration, extending infinitely so that the cinema's aura of cancelled film images, corporeal presences and acts of vision all intensify to constitute the raw material that remains archived away, for future re-discovery, in that enclosed, locked-down space. But abandoned cinemas may also be adapted, re-used, overruled, becoming the venues for activities which may appear antithetical to the filmic origin of the space, but which remain ineradicably inflected by cinematic obsession, and by its death. That re-using of the end of film perversely enhances the space's aura of abandonment still further, whatever form that re-usage takes – with the cinemas of Los Angeles's Broadway, of mutations into the forms of plasma-television storage-spaces, music-venues, sex-clubs, churches, or into momentary post-filmic apparitions, such as the Club Silencio in *Mulholland Drive*. The broader and more oblivious those strategies of re-usage appear, the greater that space remains seminally determined by its origination in film. The cultural historian Giuliana Bruno charted the re-using of New York's original cinemas, and noted that she 'encountered a veritable map of metamorphosis. If I did not find the theaters in ruins, cut up into multiplexes, or transformed from a cinematic temple into the sanctuary of a church, I found myself in such establishments as a supermarket, a restaurant, or even a university cafeteria.'[10] Bruno makes the point that the re-usage of a cinema as a multiplex does not constitute a progressive adaptation, but rather a fundamental breakage in the forms of visual media (whereas the re-usage of cinematic space for that of religious events implies a degree of transition, even if only in the endurance of sensory compulsion and emotional delirium, directed by that space's spectators towards the omniscient region of the screen). Even cinemas which have been demolished and appear to be comprehensively wiped from the map, their voided space re-used from a zero-point, almost invariably leave behind some ignitable fragment of memory, which can then magnify and reanimate itself, like an alien's residual fluid-trace in a horror-film, to engulf the entirety of filmic memory.

The extreme instance of that strategy of re-usage lies in connection with a city's first constructed cinema, or in the case of cities whose first cinema has been obliterated, the first cinema which still survives. In Lisbon that initiatory cinema is the Animatógrafo do Rossio, constructed in 1907 in the narrow Rua dos Sapateiros, off the Rossio square. Archival images of the cinema at that time show its Art Nouveau facade with a doorway on the right for spectators to enter, and a doorway on the left for spectators to leave, each supervised by immaculately uniformed ushers. Between those doorways, above a ticket-kiosk built into the cinema's facade, a metallic, royal-blue rectangle marked 'programma' could be inscribed in chalk with each day's projections, with spaces for compact posters on either side. Over a century later, that facade remained almost identical, as though effortlessly defying film's end. The doorways on either side of the ticket-kiosk were now thickly curtained,

Animatógrafo do Rossio facade.

with ecstatic cries penetrating the curtains' gaps, and led immediately into the darkness of the auditorium without the transition
of a foyer. In the 1980s, during the period when the cinemas of
Los Angeles's Broadway lapsed from showing pornography into
utter dereliction, the Animatógrafo do Rossio ceased programming
feature films and began showing pornography, moving from celluloid to video to digital projection. Since the supreme, all-
consuming domain of pornography is now that of digital media,
the obsolete persistence of a still-cinematic, seemingly ineradicable
pornographic space constituted a temporal aberration whose form
served to embody and enhance the abandonment of film. Inside
the auditorium, most of the scattered, solitary spectators appeared
concentrated on the convulsing figures on the battered, minuscule
screen, though furtive activities performed at the auditorium's
peripheries indicated a degree of distraction, in that originating
space of film, intimating that at least some of the corporeal obsessions associated with cinematic space remained intact, at film's end.

Film's first cinemas – when they survive, in a state of lavish
ruination or despoilment, as with Lisbon's Animatógrafo do Rossio
and the cinemas of Los Angeles's Broadway – display the impact of
abandonment in its most unadulterated state, whether that abandonment manifests itself in an apparently infinite limbo of oblivion

and neglect, thereby creating unique zones for the exploration of film's end, or whether the cinemas have been subjected to strategies of re-use that invariably serve only to impart an increased volatility and intensity to those spaces' skinned-alive cinematic traces. First cinemas also carry the enveloping aura of a fall into darkness, which intimates the spectatorial self-abandonment, of human senses and vision, integral to film's power, even beyond its end.

PART 2

ABANDONED IMAGES

Los Angeles Broadway 2

From the pavement outside the Million Dollar Theater, the facades of the abandoned cinemas of Broadway can be dissected by the eye from the avenue's other facades and signs: a multiplicity of hoardings, billboards, shopfronts, tea-painted brickwork, much of it left over from companies that ceased to exist decades ago, and cohered by the extravagant exclamations of spray-can graffiti. The Million Dollar Theater forms the northernmost cinema on Broadway, with the eleven other abandoned cinemas scattered along both sides of the avenue for a mile or so, all the way down to the United Artists Theater at its southernmost extremity. In some cases, the vertical signs of the cinemas remain intact in their ruination, too prominent or embedded into the urban fabric to be dismantled; other signs have become overlayered, adapted or part-hidden by the insignia of their buildings' new proprietors, though all may be caught by the eye, as elements so obsolete within the contemporary moment that they remain poised on the precipice of invisibility or obliteration, but which perversely hold their ground. Flying north to south above the Broadway avenue, via helicopter, the prominent, near-corporeal masses of the cinemas' auditoria appear far more visibly than at ground-level – forming spatial puncture-points from overhead, magnified alongside the smaller, adjacent office buildings

Million Dollar Theater facade.

and derelict department stores – since those auditoria often remain near-virtual presences from ground level, concealed behind their facades, or camouflaged by the surrounding buildings; the forms of those auditoria are revealed only by an omniscient, vertical perspective, like that carried by innumerable films, such as *Mulholland Drive* and *Blade Runner*, which survey Los Angeles and its avenues from overhead, as though to touch or enter that space will incite dangerous sensations. But the abandoned cinemas of Broadway can only be entered from ground level, through an excavation of the genealogies of film's ruination.

The interior of the Million Dollar Theater exhaled that ruination in its purest sensory form, since the seats of its balcony and stalls remained intact, allowing a suspended filmic presence to permeate that space, as though it had poised itself indefinitely at the split-second after its abandonment, though its projectors and screen had disappeared. At the time of its construction, in 1918, the cinema was vaunted as being luxurious and technologically adept beyond all previous cinemas, with the (invented) price of its construction adopted as its name as a maximal limit to inspire awe; the immense concrete girder supporting its sweeping balcony formed an unprecedented innovation in cinema engineering, and the intricate spatial arrangement of its decorative elements articulated an entire narrative, derived from a children's fairytale about wealth and generosity. In its palpable aura of death (noted by Wilson in *In Search of a Midnight Kiss*, as he and Vivian enter the cinema), that interior possessed a whirling vertigo of memory, constellated by all of the filmic sensations ever unleashed in that space, and exacerbated by those imageries' cancellation. The balcony's fire-doors remained open, so that narrow searchlights of overheated Broadway air traversed the space, illuminating fragments of disintegration on its carved walls and now-fissured ceiling. In the cinema's foyer, faded posters of Mexican filmstars carried the memory-trace of its

Blade Runner, 1982.

history as a prominent venue for Spanish-language films – one of its multiple inhabitations across the impoverished decades, once Hollywood's preferred cinemas were no longer those of Broadway – with that memory-trace preserved through the cinema's occasional contemporary use as a raucous venue for performances by *mariachi* bands from Sinaloa and other Mexican provinces, between long intervals of silence.

During its terminal cinematic era of projecting Spanish-language films, often those drawn from exploitation or horror genres, the illuminated facade of the Million Dollar Theater became enmeshed into Ridley Scott's film *Blade Runner* (1982), in which the genetic engineer J. F. Sebastian inhabits the otherwise empty Bradbury Building, an extraordinary office-complex constructed in sandstone in 1893,

25 years before the Million Dollar Theater was built, directly opposite, on the far side of Broadway. In *Blade Runner*, set in 2019, the
Bradbury Building's interior perpetually streams with water from
Los Angeles's now incessant rainstorms, and its entrance is part-
blocked by debris, within which the replicant Pris hides in order to
surprise Sebastian as he returns from work. Later in the film, the
blade-runner Deckard arrives at the Bradbury Building for his encounter with Pris and the replicants' memory-haunted leader, Roy,
who dies on the roof of an adjacent building. In both sequences, the
Million Dollar Theater's facade is prominently visible.[1] An astonishing survival of film manifests itself in those images: in the technologically supreme, though also irreparably ruined, filmic moment
of 2019 – in which Los Angeles's Downtown and Chinatown districts
have acquired the immense image-screens, concentrated street-
signage and sonic furore of Tokyo's Shinjuku district – the Million
Dollar Theater has somehow endured, and is still tenaciously
projecting to its spectators its last-ditch Spanish-language films of
1982. In *Blade Runner*, the presence of the Million Dollar Theater
forms an acute anachronism that is also an essential filmic presence,
like Deckard's reading of printed newspapers in the digitized city,
or Dr Chew's strangely artisanal workshop-production of eyes
for the genetically sophisticated, near-flawless replicants. But the
existence of those two conflictual filmic moments in *Blade Runner* –
1982 and 2019 – also serves to intimate the experience of a simultaneous presence of seemingly-opposed moments of film, within
the contemporary form of Los Angeles. In a temporal anomaly generated by the abandonment of Broadway's cinemas, the instant of
the origination of those cinemas, together with their moments of
glory and gradual dereliction, and of their final entry into infinite
destitution, all manifest themselves at will, beyond the linearity of
time, which itself careers forwards and backwards, in that aberrantly
film-inflected urban zone.

Further down Broadway from the Million Dollar Theater, the next two abandoned cinemas form another temporal anomaly: the avenue's first-constructed and last-constructed cinemas, the Roxie and the Cameo, from 1910 and 1931, are juxtaposed side by side, with no spatial interval between them. On a vast advertising hoarding above the Cameo's facade, an angel with closed eyes appeared, and, on the same surface, in place of the absent name of the angel's corporate proprietor, a seven-foot-high graffiti inscription: 'INSANER'. The cinema's marquee, with the still-illuminated lettering of its name, had meshed with the multiple signs of the building's re-use; its foyer was occupied by a store selling plasma televisions and other digital artefacts, their sale propelled by fast-talking Mexican men. Behind the store, a plywood door led into the auditorium of the Cameo. Like other first cinemas, at the moments of their end, such as the Animató-grafo do Rossio in Lisbon, the Cameo formed an engulfing presence, as though it still held the power to originate or transform human vision. That interior was now saturated with cardboard boxes holding digital televisions, stacked up high in the area that had once held the seats of the cinema's stalls, as though it were only natural that the terminal confrontation of the filmic and the digital should take place in the arena of an originating cinema. The fabric of the auditorium had deteriorated to an extreme point: cracked apart into ruination in its neglect, and illuminated only by a few bare lightbulbs among the cardboard boxes. From the viewpoint of the raised platform where the now-vanished screen had once stood, the cinema's balcony area was visible, high above, the seats still there, surrounded by railings installed during its last moment of cinematic operation, three decades or so earlier, but the balcony's walls had partly fallen in, leaving voids in space, and the once-ornamental ceiling appeared blackened by decay. The Cameo's silent space transmitted a raw cacophony of memory, and the strange sensory aura of exhilaration that always accompanies filmic abandonment.

Cameo cinema facade.

The Memory of Film

Abandoned cinemas form experimental laboratories for the memory of film: not only for a ghostly inhabitation by memory, but as spaces in which the future forms of memory may be determined, since the nature of memory, in the digital era, undergoes a fundamental transmutation, exacerbated by its separation from a century-long intimate rapport with film's imageries, which preeminently created and initiated memory. The preoccupation with the fabrication of memory in Blade Runner notably haunts its spectators; the replicant Rachael's childhood memories are stored within photographic images which she angrily discards on realizing their fraudulence, and only Roy's memories – uniquely corporeal and ocular ones, of planetary spectacle and combat, and transmitted only once, to the blade-runner Deckard, immediately before their evanescing ('all those moments will be lost in time, like tears in rain') at the moment of Roy's death – form authentic media of memory for the future. The resonance of Blade Runner progressively expands for its spectators, over the decades since its production, across the digital era, since its obsession with memory increasingly enters a temporal domain where memory becomes ever more precarious, subject to forcible deletion or replication. In film's abandonment, its cinematic spaces still hold the infinity of their memories, together with the sensory experiences initiated by memory, in an intensive form, since the provisional moment of abandonment may expire at any time, into erasure; the pressurized concentration of memory, within that sustained moment of abandonment, generates the irreplicable volatility that renders such cinematic memories prescient ones, for the future of visual memory.

The cultural experience of filmic images and of cinemagoing, during an extended historical period, directed and inflected many or all of the ways of living and ways of perceiving of populations worldwide, who learned to remember filmically, within the narrative-forms and visual cadences of film, just as they dreamed filmically, and reached the end of a dream in the same way that they experienced a film's end, as an abrupt, concerted moment of abandonment; film always generated the processes of a mass dreaming, rather than simulating them. The memory of film became so integrally bound-up with the nature of memory itself that the lapsing or vanishing of film, at its death, may constitute an essential trauma of memory, requiring attempts at sensory compensation through the transformation of the memory of film into other, disparate media forms, and into the human perception of contemporary environments as necessarily despoiled, post-filmic locations. In that sense, the spaces of film's abandonment, such as its derelict cinemas, may often appear to be the sole surviving intact spaces, with a direct and tangible access to memory, within a city, whose surrounding spaces, inhabited by an engulfing corporate image culture, then become those of a voiding of memory. But even the historical memory of the powerful human attachment to film and to cinemagoing is a fragile one, sustained (once the sensory experience of its spectators becomes lost in time) by documents and archives – such as photographs of audiences in film-palaces and drive-ins, or in the improvised spaces of experimental cinema – that are as subject to undifferentiated modification and erasure as all other images.

An integral element of film's powerful memory is connected to the ways in which its industries worked to comprehensively shape and overhaul human gesture, behaviour and corporeality, alongside sensory and emotional experience. From its origins, film inducted its audiences into ways of understanding and adapting to rapid cultural and social change, as with the travelling film-shows of the 1910s and '20s that toured rural areas without cinemas, in the USA, Europe and Asian countries such as Japan, operated by itinerant showmen who simply pitched a tent to screen their films or else projected them in the open air after dark, and which revealed to those rural audiences that urban populations possessed an entirely different set of gestures to their own: beguiling gestures which could be adopted and inhabited, notably through an abandonment of rural life and relocation to metropolitan environments. The same process of the memorization of film's gestural imperatives operated too in an urban context, especially for immigrant populations newly arrived in the usa during the same period. Film propelled its initially disparate, disorderly spectators into assuming new forms of behaviour and of spatial positioning, both within the urban environment and within the cinema's auditorium itself; as the film historian Miriam Hansen notes,

> The elaboration of classical methods of spectator-positioning appears as the industrial response to the problems posed by the cinema's availability to ethnically diverse, socially unruly, and sexually mixed audiences . . . The 'proper' relations among viewer, projector, and screen, the peculiar dimensions of cinematic space, were part of a cultural practice that had to be learned.[2]

After the consolidation of the Hollywood industry and its adoption of sound technology, its films worked pre-eminently to demonstrate the fascination of gestures, substantiated by fashion or by the aura of violence and sexual attraction, that could be committed to memory, along with the distinctive voices of film stars, then assimilated and embodied by their audiences: memories of film made flesh.

An audience's embodiment of film's memory could also, conversely, become a disruptive one, extending far beyond the boundaries of cinema spaces and insurging into the surrounding urban environments, from the Tokyo gang-cultures attracted to the glacial gestures of Mifune's white-suited gangster Matsunaga in Kurosawa's *Drunken Angel* (1948), to the American motorcycle cultures fixated on Brando's gestures of nihilism in *The Wild One* (1953). The ephemerality of filmic fashions, perpetually amended or consigned to oblivion by film industry priorities, imparted an inverse tenacity and endurance to their audiences' film-derived gestures and corporeal obsessions. Cinematic space both originated and constituted the site of intricate ritual gestures, with cinemas' role as a privileged arena for sexual acts forming one particular dimension of the entire gestural vocabulary of inhabiting a cinema. The cinema riots of eras of political protest, especially in the late 1960s, or during all-night cult-movie screenings in subsequent decades, demonstrated that a set of gestures could be formulated and performed in cinematic space, but also destroyed, in uproar.

Cinema's Freezing

The multiple forms of the disruption of cinematic space may be performed in a range of ways: as an element of collective political protest, notably that undertaken worldwide in the late 1960s; or through the drug-fuelled violence of all-night cult-movie elation, such as that of the Broadway cinemas' terminal era of the 1970s and '80s; but also as an intentional artistic strategy, as in the Lettrist art movement's experimental provocations and negations of cinematic space, entailing physical assaults on their films' assembled spectators, and disruptions of the film-projection process itself, staged in Paris in the early 1950s, at the screenings of works such as Isidore Isou's *On Venom and Drool* (1951) and Maurice Lemaître's *Has the Film Already Started?* (1952). The Lettrist movement (a dissident splinter of which later became the Situationist movement) envisaged ideal screening events at which the audience would be made to wait interminably outside the cinema while being insulted by its proprietor and doused with buckets of icy water; once inside, the projection would be incessantly disrupted and the screen assaulted. Finally, the filmmaker would capriciously decide not to project the final reel of the film, creating further uproar, and leading to a mass arrest of the audience by the police. Lemaître wrote of the need 'to break out of, to explode the normal framework of cinematographic representation', by implementing the 'destruction of the screen in its existing form and research into possibilities for the advent of a new screen'.[3] In their divergent ways, such enactments of cinematic disquiet across the second half of the twentieth century may all articulate unease at the incipient erasure of cinematic space itself, and constitute responses to it, whether through protest at power formations which habitually employed media other than that of cinema (television above all, before the digital image) for their consolidation, or in a Rimbaudian, nihilistic exhilaration at film's ruination, or through the form of artistic interventions that explored how the fascination attached to cinema could be dissected and undone. The profound mass-cultural experience of film and of cinema-going accumulated such pervasiveness within human gesture and perception across the decades following the 1920s that its eventual dissolution necessarily possessed a correspondingly deep, sensorial and corporeal crash.

Since film's memory attaches itself to images, and to the sensations emanating from those images, the cancellation or refiguring of those images entails an erosion of the processes of memory itself. Memory becomes a different entity, in which the search for a focus of memory in the film images which previously sustained and substantiated it may still be performed, but the images at stake have now vanished. The process by which the seizing of one memory then activates the search for another memory, to assemble sequences of memories (the forms of which, in the era of film, habituated themselves to adopting the forms of filmic sequences) is also one subject to incessant collapse once film is ended. Filmic memory becomes a phenomenon which compulsively misfires, in the same way that a corrupted technology cannot be successfully activated. Cinemas provided protectively cordoned spaces for memory in which a film's narrative form often allowed the opportunity for memory to detach itself from that linear narrative and pursue its own tangential trajectories, of memory-impelled detours and ellipses, for the duration of the film (ineptly constructed B-movies and easily assimilated genre films both inspired reverence in film audiences, since their forms imparted the maximum autonomy to spectators to create parallel universes of memory sequences, from the initial stimuli of the film's formulaic and therefore infinitely malleable, adaptable imageries). At film's end, memory may enter a sclerotic state in which the media images that engulf it entirely lack the activating capacity of film.

The human eye undergoes a similar response to that of memory, in its withdrawal from film, since the eye's operation is also subject to an acute habituation that can take on an addictive form in its relationship with film. The eye's vulnerable activity is figured compulsively within the narratives of film, as a seminal presence, through close-ups of the eye as the organ that serves to initiate filmic vision, whose pupil directly intimates the impact of an act or spectacle on the human body to which that eye is attached (often, a sensory impact, of ecstasy, or terror), and whose momentary averting indicates that something is unviewable, beyond the endurance of vision. The eye forms an axis of filmic fascination, but it is also a self-willed, aberrant organ in its relationship with film; despite the cinematic resonances of its components' namings – the iris, macula, retina, sclera, pupil – and its intricate systems for the registration and processing of images, the eye bears only a surface rapport to the forms and technologies of the film camera, film-projector and cinema screen. The eye's depths entirely elude

Un Chien Andalou,
1929.

film, even when, as at the opening of Buñuel's *Un Chien Andalou*,
the eye is cinematically razored open, to unleash its mysteries.

The corporeal experience at film's end parallels the vertiginous
disorientation of the eye, which remains in memory-like flux as it
addictively searches for its sustaining focus in film, but is unable to
locate it. Across its history, film fixed the body into multiple intervals of stasis (as in the luxurious waiting-salons of the Kino Riga,
where spectators reclined in immobility, anticipating the subsequent incapacitation to be experienced in the auditorium, for the
film-screening's duration), but also impelled its spectators into
movement, into unknown areas, from its earliest moments, when
films shot from a viewpoint at the front of moving trains, as with the
Lumière Brothers' travel-films of the late 1890s, enabled spectators
to experience a corporeal propulsion into unforeseen terrains and
panoramas. The cinematic venture known as Hale's Tours, whose
variants became immensely popular in amusement parks worldwide
around 1906, literally shook and animated its spectators by design-
ing the cinematic space as that of a carriage whose movement replicated the jolts and seisms of exploratory journeys; that erratic motion
had an intentionally corporeal impact, as Lauren Rabinovitz notes:

'The first travel ride films simulated railroad or auto travel in order to foreground the body itself as a site for sensory experience.'[4] Throughout its subsequent history, film always entailed an unleashing of vision that encompassed and compacted together the eye and the body. For many die-hard ex-inhabitants of film, the cancellation of its spaces demands a corporeal transmutation into incessant movements through the space of cities, to pinpoint film locations, to overlayer an existing architecture with a filmic architecture, or to undertake random trajectories designed to conjure filmic memories. At film's end, the experience of its progressive running down, into dereliction, often possessed a direct correspondence to the human body's own operation: in many last-ditch cinemas, on the point of financial meltdown and abandonment, the auditorium's heating system became deactivated or malfunctioned, and spectators endured the time of film in a perceptually concentrated form, in which the plummeting of body temperature paralleled the time of film's own decline, before the terminal freezing of film. An especially resonant space for frozen-to-death cinema is that of Eye World, the laboratory of Dr Chew in *Blade Runner*, whose insignia-marked, cinemalike facade hides a glacial interior in which sub-zero working conditions need to be maintained in order to generate the capacity for vision of the replicants' eyes created there. Eye World forms an open, revelatory space that may easily be entered in order to extract essential data about time or identity, but that is also a precarious, unsustainable space; the human body's inhabitation of that extreme domain must be a transient one.

Underground Cinema

The essential transience of the experience of film, at its ending, may involve the inhabitation of uncertain spaces from which most of the tangible evidence of film has disappeared, and only a hallucinatory filmic aura endures. At the geographical heart of film's greatest historical hallucination, that of Hollywood, many of the cinemas constructed in the 1920s and '30s along Hollywood Boulevard (thereby consigning the cinemas of the Broadway area of Los Angeles's Downtown to eventual oblivion) are now demolished, or turned into cultist churches. But deep below the ground, the grandiose aura of cinema survives in the form of the Hollywood and Vine metro station, opened in 1999 and designed to replicate a film-palace from Hollywood's era of glory, with an architecture recalling the terracotta-tile facades and interior walls of cinemas, together with subdued lighting that evokes the moment before a cinema's plunge into darkness for the start of a film, and exit doors and passageways in the style of those of cinemas. The vaulted roof of the station's platforms is entirely covered with many thousands of empty film reels, and a space is set aside for the display of

Hollywood and Vine metro station.

obsolete film-projectors. The station's corridors are embedded with fragments of images and texts evoking the zenith of Hollywood's industry, together with the tenuous passages of human figures through that industry: passages often with a brutal transience of their own, engendering the film suicides and murders which Kenneth Anger lovingly documented in his book *Hollywood Babylon*, and which David Lynch explores in *Mulholland Drive*. In that subterranean space, all that remains is the fragile edifice of film, with no core, like the ruined rural drive-in cinemas that can occasionally be glimpsed alongside California's freeways, with only their vast wooden facades remaining, the lettering now faded to a point only a hairsbreadth to the side of legibility, and with the spaces behind those ramshackle facades, for spectators' cars and the drive-ins' colossal screens, now entirely voided. In the Hollywood and Vine metro station, film's mutated presence is experienced transiently, as vagrants and commuters pass through at speeds that vary like those of film projection (16 or 24 frames a second), the phantasmagorical residue of film caught only in their peripheral vision. Film has been literally expunged from the face of the city, to be consigned underground.

In its abandonment, film may take on a subterranean form, as with the Hollywood and Vine metro station, thereby constituting a contemporary variant of 'underground cinema' that intersects, if only in its outlandish form and virtual dynamics, with the experimental film movements and individual film artists of the 1950s and '60s (including prominent figures such as Stan Brakhage, Jonas Mekas and, again, Anger) who were collectively named, by the writer Manny Farber, 'Underground Cinema': an approach to filmmaking that often possessed an explicit hostility to Hollywood, rejecting the homogeneous industrial formations of film and their fixed narratives, and experimenting instead with alternative ways to conjure vision, desire and the tangible immediacy of film's impacts, as though film's history could still be erased and re-started from zero, with new spaces of projection (alongside a network of independent cinemas that operated in autonomy from those owned by film studios or distribution conglomerates, Underground Cinema's screenings often took place in improvised spaces such as nightclubs and hotel rooms, sometimes covertly, to avoid police raids and imprisonment whenever the films' distinctive sexual or political content had contravened censorship laws). Underground Cinema's alternative pioneers, sixty or more years after Muybridge, Le Prince and the Skladanowsky Brothers, often exhibited the same passion for factional infighting as their predecessors, though entities such as Jonas Mekas's New York Film-Makers' Cooperative created a rare collaborative equanimity in Underground Cinema's history. Many of the preoccupations of Underground Cinema, with the potential for spatial, visual and corporeal transformations exacted by the medium of film, now re-manifest themselves at the moment of film's abandonment, since the processes of dereliction and disintegration integral to abandonment entail a fundamental overhauling or cancellation of the nature of film and its industrial formations, and also intensify the temporal impacts of film into the forms of sensorial immediacy and of residual, anti-narrational images – always pivoting around the human body and its visual capacities – that had been envisaged by Underground Cinema's pioneers of the 1950s.

At film's end, the entirety of filmic history appears as a vastly expansive but also calamitous hallucination emanating from the geographical axis of Hollywood, and which compacts infinite proliferation with self-willed erasure. In that sense, alongside the abandoned cinemas of Broadway and underground film-bunkers such as the Hollywood and Vine metro station, film also possesses an afterlife as hallucinatory landscape, evident pre-eminently in the raw, despoiled urban panoramas of Hollywood, visible from vantage-points such as Mulholland Drive, and within filmically inflected landscapes such as that of Zabriskie Point. When an all-consuming hallucination evanesces, or has been gratuitously supplanted, its residue may take on a form in inverse proportion to the cultural magnitude of its original manifestation. The sparse traces of cinema, perceptible in landscape through a visual obsession that searches out and amasses those traces into an archive of film's disappearance, may be located both scattered on urban surfaces and also underground, like archaeological debris. If such an archive of the post-filmic could be brought into being, it might begin with a film-narrational opening which then remained unclosable, suspended like the aura of abandonment projected by the Broadway cinemas: Once, film no longer existed.

Cinema's Legibility

In the uncertain spaces generated by film's abandonment, unprecedented forms of cinematic language may emerge from within the disintegration of filmic traces. From the 1920s onwards, following a period of rapid transition between the temporary forms of nickelodeons and storefront projection-rooms, cinemas began to be designed as immovable architectural entities, intended to survive for as long as they could generate income for their proprietors, and often inbuilt with the capacity for modification and transformation as the technologies of film advanced; as a result, the infrastructure and exterior facades of abandoned cinemas often emanate a stubborn endurance, even when those spaces have been derelict for several decades. They resistantly transmit a permanent language of film, even when that language can no longer be understood; their marquees and signs may remain intact, though the information they exclaim into the surrounding urban environment has often been annulled or emptied out. Even when their marquees become multilingual concoctions, pitched between the cinemas' original names and the content of posters or hoardings promoting the plasma-television stores, nightclubs or churches that now occupy their interiors, as with the derelict cinemas of Broadway, it is always the filmic component of language that retains the upper hand.

But the language of abandoned cinemas' facades may also erode to a near-terminal point, as with the facades of long-redundant drive-in cinemas whose wooden hoardings' near-illegible content may be reduced to a single identifiable word: 'drive-in'. Without that one last distinguishing word, those cinemas would lapse, mutating into enigmatic, opaque formations in the landscape, like millennia-old dolmens. Especially within the peripheral areas of cities, that precipice of cinematic legibility may contain the elements of a fragmentary language of film's survival. In the strange marine landscape south of San Francisco's airport, the late-1960s Hyatt cinema appears marooned in an immense, empty car park, its extravagant architecture combining the forms of an eastern European 'palace of culture' with that of an interplanetary spaceship, the roof surmounted by an inverted lunar module. On the bayside highway, a sign announces that the ruined cinema can be leased, but the telephone number provided is one with a defunct code, and that sign is overshadowed by vast digital screens displaying locked images of traffic stasis. The windows of the cinema's box-office are haphazardly boarded over with different-sized pieces of wood, as though its oblivious neglect extended even into the act of its abandonment. Many abandoned cinemas worldwide appear to have been vacated with inexplicable urgency, in great haste, with half-consumed drinks-cans left behind in the foyers, intimate possessions strewn on the floors, film-cans scattered around the projection-boxes, and vending machines left switched on, as though those cinemas' proprietors and final audiences had been led away without warning by a Stalinist secret police. The Hyatt's hoardings for the announcement of current films and

Hyatt cinema box-office.

Hyatt cinema
eroded hoarding.

forthcoming attractions, or other information necessary for its
spectators, are now deteriorated to the point of virtual illegibility,
an encroaching black fog of fungal erasure leaving only the barest
shards of filmic data, like a debris of hieroglyphs: the number '20'
appears to be present, but may equally be the first letters of a word
beginning 'zo', and several other isolated sequences of letters may
be interpreted. An intensive process of reconstruction, oscillating
between the visual and the memorial, is required for that linguistic autopsy, whose results will be flawed, if any solution at all can
be revealed. The linguistic elements by which film may be known
become radically disassembled by the process of cinematic abandonment; film's language appears irretrievably lost.

But in that loss, film's language is also liberated, and its erased elements may be rewritten or imagined from zero. Surfaces in the interiors of many abandoned cinemas are covered with spray-can or marker-pen graffiti by intruders, so that those surfaces (especially those of the box office and projection-room) become saturated with complex, multilayered inscriptions. Not only walls, but cinematic debris such as the remaining fragments of the screen, metallic editing tables left behind in projection-boxes, and even the cinemas' terrazzo flooring, form sensitized media for those inscriptions, which often register the names and postcodes of intruders, recount sexual acts undertaken there, or obsessively give precise dates, often future, impossible dates, for their entry into that cinematic space, as though providing a linguistic verification that the corporeal inhabitation of that space remains viable. Just as the proprietors of the newly constructed cinemas of the 1920s and '30s habitually lauded the architectural glory and technological innovations of their cinemas in press advertisements, so momentary intruders into abandoned cinematic space mark its terminal downfall in intricate graffiti sequences.

The language of cinema, at its end, is one that often inhabits and anatomizes a precarious, ambivalent temporal boundary between the filmic and the digital, or between memory and oblivion. But once a cinema has lost the entirety of its insignia and traces, it may also irrevocably lose its spatial legibility within the city that surrounds it, and, in an extreme instance, become impossible to distinguish from, for example, a former department store or any other building requiring a large open space at ground-level. Cinemas may also have been comprehensively razed, to the last recognizable detail, either by fire or through their vulnerability to damage from earthquakes or other calamities. This process of the utter erasure of film's traces previously occurred, in a concentrated timespan, when nickelodeons (small, basic and often dangerous spaces for film projection, mainly converted from shops, and massively popular worldwide between 1905 and 1915) abruptly disappeared, as Maggie Valentine notes: 'Overshadowed, outclassed, and physically dwarfed by the larger and more pretentious movie palaces being built by the mid-1910s, most nickelodeons were eventually converted back into restaurants, hardware stores, cigar stores, and haberdasheries.'5 The contemporary vanishing into space of cinemas forms a different proposition; once their last identifiable filmic trace has apparently become detached, those cinemas lose even their sustaining aura of abandonment, slipping beyond language. In such cases, the relocation of any linguistic trace or fragment of an erased cinema forms a revelatory restitution.

Film's End and the Digital

The extinguishing of film's spaces, in their moment of abandonment, contrarily engenders a distinctive presence of film, with cinematic traces still recoverable as open media for the envisioning of new visual forms, as long as those neglected spaces have eluded a definitive erasure. But film and its spaces may also be actively supplanted by the digital, as though film had arbitrarily relinquished the status it held for a century or so as the primary visual medium for human perception and gesture, and ceded to the digital, thereby transplanting itself within the all-enveloping edifice of the digital as a minor, subsidiary partner, whose spaces could (instead of being abandoned) be upgraded into multiplexes with digital projection, and whose processes of production could now entail the digital recording, editing and distribution of what had previously been filmic images. Such a linear process of adaptation would assume that a clear temporal evolution had taken place, beginning with the widespread application of computer technology in the 1980s and concluding with the pervasiveness within human culture of the digital in the 2000s, with the intervening timespan constituting a unique zone of transmutation. But film never operated in a linear way, and its multiple histories invariably transmit an aura of interruptions, intransigent self-destructions and aberrant tangential movements, so that the relationship between the filmic and the digital constitutes a more intricate one than initially appears. It may be that film lures the digital into a position of apparent supremacy, in order to undermine it and demonstrate the vacuity of its images, thereby precipitating the desire for unprecedented post-cinematic forms.

Digital art achieved its prominence across the 1980s and '90s largely through its tension and preoccupation with film, and through the air of innovation it generated as an entity that intimated an upheaval in all forms of media, communications and art. Worldwide centres of digital art, such as ZKM in Karlsruhe and the NTT InterCommunication Center in Tokyo, focused their attention on examining the shifting dimensions of the digital, notably in the form of installation works (with a particular star-system hierarchy of practitioners and exhibitors, drawing on that of cinema's industries), and also on exploring the concurrent disintegration of film. Many digital artworks of the 1990s, such as those of Kenji Yanobe and Teiji Furuhashi, used their medium to analyse film's erosion. But, once film appears to have become definitively redundant and obsolete, it can no longer form a compelling preoccupation or subject-matter of digital art, since film's moribund presence cannot generate a vital tension with the digital image. As a result, digital art's practitioners now encounter a situation in which the art form's legibility becomes impaired; the digital and its visual language can no longer be conceived or read, since the component that pre-eminently focused that reading – the film image – has evanesced, and the digital consequently takes on a similar status to those abandoned cinemas from which all defining evidence of film has been comprehensively erased, and which can no longer be identified. Once everything has become digitized, throughout all media forms and their engulfing of all human perception and acts, the digital can no longer be effectively defined, since it cannot delimit itself against any other entity, and has no compelling content of its own (at least, not one with the capacity to engender the fascinations and obsessions ignited by film's content); it projects itself purely as stultified corporate power. In Wong Kar-Wai's film 2046 (2004), in which melancholy characters take high-speed train journeys between memory and oblivion, the final images display an entirely digitized, illegible megalopolis, located somewhere in East Asia, and which exists only to convey itself, and await its own crash.

Film possessed the capacity to probe and visualize the digital world, as 2046 does through its images of a petrified, opaque cityscape of saturated corporate image-screens and flickering megastructures: a city that is mysterious, but void. However, after film's end, that kind of exploratory rendering of the digital by film may lose the capacity it had previously held – through its positioning at a revealing interval from the digital (an interval still tangible in 2046) – to focus upon its subject, and instead appears subsumed and assimilated by that subject, so that all that remains is the digital itself. Along with the cancellation of the particular sensations and perceptions associated with film, that subsuming also annuls the capacity for the demonstration of first and last images, which was always a distinctive trait of film. Throughout its existence, film worked to pinpoint origins, along with the ellipses and collapses of time which themselves constitute originating and terminating points; notably, at a film's end, its narrative signalled an intensification of action and gesture in order to alert its spectators to the increased attention required to seize that ending, even though the narrative might remain open-ended. But in the digital era, origins and endings disappear, since no visual or narrative system exists to project anything other than the continuum that sustains digital communication, commerce and power; whenever an intimation of crisis or malfunction appears within the digital, it cannot narrate a gradual process of resolution to its consumers or spectators (in the way that film could always conjure a narrative resolution, however strange or miraculous), and instead immediately emanates an aura of meltdown and incipient apocalypse.

Film's Excess

Film's first and last images focus above all on the human body, notably on its origins and ends, just as the inhabitation of cinematic space was always primarily a corporeal one, composed of sensations precipitated by the experience of film (in the case of the film-palaces of the 1920s and '30s, an inhabitation sensorially exacerbated by the outlandish spectacle of the environment enclosing those cinemas' audiences). From its own origins, film charted the human gestures that initiated vital acts, especially those of death, sexual desire and conflict, and carried that exploration through to the gestures that marked the terminal points of those acts. At moments of social fracture, when a particular power structure or cultural formation lapsed and a disparate entity emerged, often with violence, film – especially documentary film – uniquely seized the transformational instants that intimated those ends and origins through images that registered the upheavals in their impact upon the corporeal, often in filmic forms that moved in excess of what could habitually be tolerated or envisaged in the perception of the human body.

In *Africa Addio* (1966), a notorious documentary film tracing the extraordinary violence pervading central Africa in the first half of the 1960s following the moment of de-colonization, the Italian filmmakers Gualtiero Jacopetti and Franco Prosperi intentionally

emphasized moments of acute disintegration and of new begin-
nings, moving abruptly from one to the other during the course of
their three years of incessant filming, crisscrossing central Africa
from Zanzibar to the Congo. The filmmakers interrogate the slaughter surrounding the European relinquishing of power, filming the
aftermaths of the final Mau Mau killings of British settlers in Kenya,
and the ensuing trials, as the exiting colonial power hurriedly enacts
ludicrous rituals to mark its farewell to Africa; the film's images
remain fixated on the human residue of the colonial collapse, in the
contortions of massacred bodies and the faces of those on trial. But
once the European colonizers have disappeared from central Africa
(or given an illusion of vanishing, as they wait to re-enact a new
variant of their power), the post-colonial countries' origins immediately fall into extreme disorder, engendering abandoned human
landscapes of extermination. Jacopetti and Prosperi film from a
helicopter as the 1964 massacre of the Muslim population of

Africa Addio, 1966.

Zanzibar takes place just below them, tracking across a panoramic oceanside landscape of figures attempting to flee their killers, before returning the next day to film the same landscape, in which the bodies of those hundreds of fleeing figures are now scattered by the ocean; during a riot in Dar-es-Salaam, the filmmakers are themselves filmed being hauled from their car to be shot in the street, and released only at the last moment when their executioners realise they are Italian, not British. At the end of the film, having compulsively mapped the chaos of multiple, almost indistinguishable conflicts, they record, as though by chance, an offhand execution by a mercenary of a rebel in a minor Congolese conflict (an act which, on the film's release, they were accused of inciting through the presence of their film-camera); film's sensitized power to register terminal moments veers into an excess that reveals the startling immediacy of human upheavals.

Alongside imageries of conflict at moments of historical transition, such as those of *Africa Addio*, film also served presciently to record the split-seconds when a culture went terminally askew, thereby creating images that indicated the origins of new cultural forms, and marked irreconcilable breaks from the past. At the Rolling Stones' open-air concert in December 1969 at the Altamont Speedway in California, one of the numerous cinematographers documenting the event, for the film *Gimme Shelter* (1970), filmed the killing of an audience member by the Hell's Angels security guards employed to oversee the concert. That moment, through its filming, notoriously underscored the abrupt overturning of the 1960s' preoccupation with pacifistic revolution into the uneasy, violent turmoil of the following decade's disillusionment and political corruption. The cinematographer Baird Bryant focused his camera on the malevolent turmoil at the front of the vast audience at Altamont, capturing images of a young audience member, Meredith Hunter (highly visible in a green suit), standing in the crowd, then unintentionally seized the image of Hunter's death, as he briefly brandished a handgun and was stabbed by one of the security guards. What initially appears as a chaotic blur of human gesture resolves itself into the irrevocable image of a surpassed culture disintegrating, through an act of death, into a darker form.

Film possessed the capacity to register not only the essential origins and end-points of the human figure, but also the moments when a pivotal transmutation occurred, in global conflict or culture, with a particular impact on the status of the corporeal. Such moments, in their seizing by film, often extend far beyond the visual image's stable parameters, and carry the aura of an unboundaried, abandoned excess, conceivable only through the medium of the film image, whether the image is recorded through obsessional determination, as with those generated by *Africa Addio*'s infernal post-colonial journeys, or else spontaneously, as with the image of sudden death in *Gimme Shelter*. Those moments' cinematic projection often unleashed extreme sensorial responses in their spectators. Film's abandoned cinematic spaces now carry those same resonances of an abrupt transformation which irresistibly propels the corporeal, and human identity, into unforeseen formations. Many of those spaces, as with the derelict cinemas of Broadway, were explicitly built with an architectural excess in mind in order to generate corporeal sensations (of luxury, of indulgence) that could not be gained by their audiences other than through their momentary inhabitation of those lavish spaces. Abandoned cinemas form an arena in which an immense, century-long sensory and emotional investment in film is terminated, but may leave behind a trace of that intensive rapport with film, in the form of a volatile, indestructible excess that endures above and beyond the rational process of ending, and remains suspended in that space in anticipation of new origins for human vision.

Apocalyptic Cinema

Film uniquely constructed an aura in which 'the end' could disallow its spectators' capacity to return to their extra-filmic lives as though nothing had happened; the narrative of those lives could not be effortlessly picked up again, beyond cinematic space, after the vertiginous disorientation and sensorial impact which film, at its moments of most acute force, imparted to its spectators' memory and corporeal identity. Abandoned cinemas, such as those of Broadway, may intimate to onlookers that a status of 'the end' has been imposed upon film, either because those spaces are no longer viable and have become obsolete, or because film has been entirely superseded by the digital. But film itself possessed an extraordinary ability to evoke a condition which could not conceivably entail a future, beyond the terminal moment which the film revealed. In films such as *Africa Addio* and *Gimme Shelter*, the historical and cultural prognosis is one that appears to exclude a future: the decolonization process has fallen into utter disintegration, and no agent exists to salvage Africa, while the 1960s American pacifistic revolutionary ideals have lapsed into such terminal violence, at the decade's end, that the envisaged future has been cancelled. Only retrospectively, several decades on, and viewed from the far side of those seemingly definitive cinematic apocalypses, can the perversity of the future's existence be perceived: African post-colonial history did persist, in slaughter, and American culture did sustain itself, in disillusioned corruption.

The cinematic experience of a film which spectacularly brings down 'the end' upon its audience's heads, with corporeal intent, is one in which the transfixed spectators habitually remain in their seats after the last image has passed, still staring at the screen, often emotionally drained or weeping, unable to face the moment at which they must abandon the cinema to resume their lives. In Coppola's

Apocalypse Now, 1979.

Apocalypse Now (1979), for example, the film entails a mysterious journey in which the familiar agents of its spectators' identification – the motley crew of Willard's patrol-boat, as he heads upriver into Cambodia, to assassinate Colonel Kurtz – are gradually subtracted by their deaths, so that the spectators' focus narrows down to that of Willard's obsession itself. The crew must perpetually scan the banks of the river to elude the gunfire or spears that will kill them, but that relentless concentration is intermittently sent reeling, into hallucination, as the crew become pitched from their boat, to experience the riot surrounding the Playboy models' performance or the equally hallucinogenic attack on the Do Long Bridge. Once Willard has reached Kurtz's compound and assassinated him, the film expands to engulf and negate the future: Willard can go no further nor travel backwards, Kurtz's city-like compound has been annulled, and the Vietnam war itself has exceeded all familiar indicators of warfare, so that Willard's act is erased within it. Even the film's sustaining napalm-fire and cacophony die away. Film creates its own apocalypse, and its spectators experience the sensorial abyss that blacks out the future.

Across its history, and notably in the science fiction and disaster genres, film figured variants of global danger in which the planet came under exterior attack and risked freezing, combusting or lapsing into stasis; its inhabitants faced being wiped out or atomized, replicated or subjugated by aliens and monsters. In most instances, a solution could be found, and the global danger passed, with the film's end, so that survival was ensured. In films of warfare, the combat habitually reaches a point at which the situation appears irrecuperable, but a strategy of courageous response eventually enables a resolution; even in a film such as Tarkovsky's *Ivan's Childhood* (1962), in which the young Soviet-army scout Ivan has been executed by the German forces at the film's end, a coda evoking his exhilarated headlong running, alongside a river's edge, allows a miraculous survival. With the rise of widespread public awareness of global climate upheaval, which coincided with the perceived 'death' of cinema and the ascendancy of the digital, in the 1990s and 2000s, film began to develop imageries of spectacular CGI-engendered apocalypses, in which the agent of the threatened apocalypse was no longer alien, or an external enemy, but self-generated and self-directed. The imminent apocalypse, though created by human acts, could still also be deferred or even readily resolved by human acts (in *The Core*, 2003, through an internal spacecraft journey, penetrating from the surface to the very heart of the planet, in order to 'right' it); but a fundamental seism had occurred in audiences' perception of a global survival that could traverse the film's end, and endure into the future, since such imageries had become jarringly mismatched with the future certainty of climatic disintegration.

Abandoned cinemas possess a space which is that of 'the end', and inhabit that space as one that is tangibly suspended in its terminal moment, and has no way forward. Those spaces also intimate a filmmaking of the same moment – the contemporary moment – in which the end-point of global survival itself becomes a matter for exploration, and a literally apocalyptic filmmaking may appear (for which Tarkovsky's films constitute a precursor) that interrogates the sensation and meaning of that ending, which is simultaneously human and filmic. That filmmaking may envision the amassed disintegration, human residues and apparitions of memory which also constellate the spaces of derelict cinemas, but it may also project the self-abandoned elation that is irresolubly welded to 'the end', to last moments and terminal events. And a contrary resolve to escape even a definitive ending, or at least to imagine such an escape from apocalypse, forms an essential component of film's aberrance, just as the painter Francis Bacon (in the final words of his interviews with David Sylvester) could reflect on his ability to elude even being irreversibly consigned to hell, noting that 'if I was in hell I would always feel I had a chance of escaping. I'd always be sure that I'd be able to escape.'[6]

Filmic Amnesia

Film's audiences, confronted with images which appeared in excess of their habitual visual and corporeal experience, underwent that contact with film as a concentrated, exceptional one, that became 'memorable', imprinted and archived in memory. Similarly, in spectacular film-palaces such as Broadway's Los Angeles Theater or the Kino Riga, during the period of those cinemas' zenith, that cinematic experience also seized memory in an exceptional way, extending beyond spectators' contacts with other media or their more habitual rapport with film in smaller, neighbourhood cinemas, in part since that exceptional experience necessitated a distinctive journey into luxury, into the heart of the city. A great collective ritual of film, on exiting a cinema or during subsequent days, among audiences worldwide, was to reconstruct the elements of a watched film in spoken language, to substantiate or dispute narrative points, to isolate and sexualize gestures, thereby embedding filmic memory still further. Once film is ended, those dual archives of memory – memories of a primary contact with now-abandoned images, and with overturned cinematic spaces – begin to lapse and to fade out, just as silent film enclosed an iris (an eye in reversal, letting in darkness) around the image, to gradually constrict it into invisibility. But the fade-out into amnesia of film may also take the contrary form adopted by Rainer Werner Fassbinder for his film *Querelle* (1982), of fading out his images not to black, but instead to blinding white light, so that the amnesia of film itself becomes an illuminatory process.

Alongside the work of remembering films, audiences devoted immense work, across many decades, to the immediate forgetting of films, in the dismissal of mundane images which provoked no sensory response, often since they belonged to genre products of no distinction, intended to maintain an industrial equilibrium; especially in the decades of the Hollywood studios' decline, generic film-industrial production became replicated by a vast audience-industry of amnesia. Spectators also consigned the film-images passing before their eyes to amnesia whenever they were preoccupied with more pressing spatial activities, such as sexual liaisons, in the era when cinematic space provided a unique exemption from familial or social strictures, so that entire films, perceived in peripheral vision, appeared barely to register; even so, isolated images, received tangentially at the boundaries of consciousness, might then perversely survive in memory, through being retrospectively welded to especially intensive or resonant corporeal acts. The fore-grounding of particular film-images, inexplicably impaled in their spectators' memory while the remainder of the film is rendered into an amnesiac blur, evokes the processes of filmic deterioration explored by Bill Morrison in his film *Decasia*, in which isolated images of brief duration have been strangely spared from the engulfing physical decomposition that has wiped out the surrounding filmic sequence so that they appear enhanced in status, as revelatory image-survivors.

Once film appears to be forgotten – and media spectators become habituated to forms of images transmitted by disparate technologies, carrying other intentions and contents – it may only resurge from its amnesia in bursts, since its familiar cinematic surroundings are obsolete, and its narratives, rhythms and durations have also been annulled. Since film was the primary medium that registered the historical and cultural events of its century of pre-eminence, those events too become subject to amnesia, since they often enmeshed themselves inextricably with film in order to elude their own forgetting, to the point that they entirely vanished into the medium of film. In his film *Sunless* (1982), Chris Marker examined the way in which particular film-images, such as those of his travels to Japan, comprehensively distilled the memory of acts, thereby protecting those acts from the process of amnesia that effortlessly consumed all other acts and their memory. Filmic amnesia may be unintentional, subject to the frailty of memory, but it can also form a determined and deliberate strategy, generating a release into the elation of forgetting, that may seek to cancel out the profound traumas closely associated with filmic experiences; the medium of film often served to initiate its young spectators into their first insights of such matters as sex and sexual acts, warfare and genocide, providing seminal and powerful imageries which often irrevocably transformed those spectators' perception and future lives, and whose trauma could be countered only by an intentional amnesia, directed against the medium of film itself. Film always formed a negative medium of exposure, integrally attached to human horror and to the fearful unknown, as well as a source of pleasurable captivation. In its capacity to resurge into memory, film may then shatter amnesia as a maleficent agent of illumination.

The processes of filmic amnesia also operate within cinematic space itself, in the forgetting of the distinctive ways in which that space was architecturally designed, constructed and inhabited; film-historians have habitually neglected those matters, and cinema-proprietors were oblivious to their documentation, with the result that cinematic space constitutes a mysterious domain.

The intricate interrelationship between the foyer, auditorium and other spaces of each of the abandoned cinemas of Los Angeles's Broadway becomes progressively more opaque without the sustaining memories of those cinemas' former audiences. The technologies of film, too, lapse into enigmas. Above all, in the digital era, when images can be mediated from any mobile surface and any source, the process of filmic projection – by which the images unravel in the projection-box located behind and above the spectators, to be dispatched over their heads, onto the screen – may become the ultimate mystery in the moment of post-filmic amnesia, just as it previously possessed its status as the initiating mystery in film history, for the pioneers of the early 1890s who knew how to record film-images, but could not devise the means to project them. The projection-box forms the originating point for every memory ever generated by film, and for those memories' sensory and corporeal consequences; but, in the amnesiac space of cinematic ruination, it is also the most intensively abandoned and unknown element.

The Mystery of Film Projection 1

The Los Angeles Theater possessed the only surviving, operational projection-box among the twelve abandoned cinemas of Broadway; in the other cinemas, the projection-box had been rendered redundant, occasionally transformed, after the end of film-projection,

into an improvised office or storage space before being comprehensively gutted, with the battered walls, as in the Rialto cinema,
still pinned with pornographic posters or long-redundant delivery
schedules, and the broken-glass-littered floors heaped with disintegrated papers and the same mixed deposits – of earth, plaster and
finely-ground brick – that comprised the sedimental landscape of
the auditorium's floor. The projection equipment of the other
cinemas was mostly long gone, broken down for last-ditch impro-
visational components to repair plasma televisions, or simply jet-
tisoned into the street as garbage (the obsolete projectors of one
moribund Los Angeles cinema had been consigned underground,
to form part of the post-cinematic decor of the Hollywood and
Vine metro station). A group of filmic die-hards conserved the
Los Angeles Theater's projection equipment in order, once each
year, to screen a single film there, to preserve the vital suspension
of cinematic abandonment's moment, their zeal indulged by the
financier-proprietor of the building. From the rear of the highest
auditorium balcony, a steep spiral staircase ascended to a cracked
doorway, and beyond that, the projection-box appeared: a long,
oblong room, thick with dust, and sunlit from the open fire-exit
at one end, which allowed the distant traffic cacophony of Broadway to bleed into the otherwise silent space. Fire-hazard signs
were everywhere, along with negligently discarded film-cans. Two
immense film-projectors subsisted from the cinema's terminal
screenings of 1980s exploitation films, though the projectors were
at least three decades older; now barely functional and requiring
extensive maintenance for their yearly reactivation, they mediated
the living coma of cinematic abandonment. Beyond those projectors, a smaller slide-projector completed the line of vision-machines,
arranged as filmic weaponry; installed at the moment of the cinema's
construction, in 1931, the slide-projector had been disused for a half-
century or more. Against the back wall, the original editing-table

had been positioned for the assembling of film-reels or for urgent repairs to celluloid that had snapped in mid-screening.

That room emanated in an intense form the mystery of film projection, of its origins and its end. It formed an edenic cinematic space, apparently created with a prescience of its own eventual redundancy in prospect, so that it could constitute a sensitized arena for inhabitation by film's ghosts, by film's end, and the ideal, incendiary-prone location for the dissolution into fragments, and incineration into ashes, of film's final detritus. At this height, the medallion-indented gilt ceiling of the cinema could be seen in detail through the projection-box window; among the terracotta figures of cherubs and naked angels, deep fissures and discoloured patches of storm-seepage constellated that golden heaven, and a calm aura of ruination hung in the air, as though the cinema tolerated its own abandonment, provided it went no further, remaining poised a hairsbreadth from erasure. Only a few lightbulbs illuminated the auditorium; the site of the curtained screen appeared infinitely distant, barely legible through the dust-whirled air, intimating the tenacious velocity required of the projectors' beams to deliver film-images to that surface.

The filmic die-hard who had shown me the projection-box explained the professional obsessionality of a projectionist's life: the amphetamine-powered twelve- or fourteen-hour shifts, arbitrarily extended whenever cinemas began to capsize financially or turned to all-night cult-film screenings; the need to keep a permanent concentration fixed on the screen, in order to maintain image-focus and ensure the reels had been assembled exactly, without narrational or sonic jolts; the extreme isolation, temperature and noise (the machinery exuded arduous heat, together with the grating cacophony of the reels passing through the projector-gate); and the relentless repetition of the same film shown for weeks on end, which contrarily provoked a strange exhilaration, rather than lassitude. Projectionists, despite their amphetamine addictions, often became profoundly silent, austere figures, with a mystery of their own, always uniquely attuned to film, their lives outside the projection-box askew or non-existent. Notably, all-night projectionists of pornography, or martial arts and exploitation films (the terminal images projected in most of the once-luxurious Broadway cinemas), bore the exacerbated corporeal traces of that exposure, notoriously resulting in film-reels shakily spliced together with a mix of adhesive tape and semen. And once those cinemas had closed down, often without warning, the physical, mental and film-memorial impact on those figures had been cruel, with the abrupt withdrawal of their obsession. Before turning to the projectors, which required intricate overhauling in advance of their once-yearly resuscitation, several months into the future, the filmic die-hard mentioned that one of the former projectionists habitually stood outside the cinema each afternoon, physically excluded from entry, and exiled in dereliction from the projection-box, since the foyer was enclosed by a metal grille.

Beyond the cinema's palatial foyer and its locked grille, a white-bearded, decrepit old man stood in isolation on the cracked terrazzo tiles (each imprinted in gold with heraldic icons of tiny flames), which extended outwards from the cinema to Broadway's traffic lanes. He held a styrofoam cup in his hand, with a few one-cent coins inside, as though he had conceived the grandiose plan, within his obsession's ruins, to collect enough money to re-open the cinema, and project any film, even ripped cuts of long-discarded, unknown celluloid from the projection-box floor, rather than nothing at all (a graffiti-scored notice secured to the grille announced the intention of converting part of the building into a 'live-work' apartment-complex). But the hand holding the cup shook so badly – like the convulsing body of Betty in Lynch's *Mulholland Drive* in her seat in the Tower cinema, transformed into the Club Silencio – that the low-value coins abruptly flew from the cup and scattered on the tiles, to be collected up by indulgent Mexican men and meticulously returned to the cup, until they were shaken out again. In both directions, the insignia of the adjacent abandoned cinemas – the Million Dollar and the Cameo to the north, the State and the Globe to the south – reproved Broadway.

State cinema marquee.

PART 3

ABANDONED EYES

Los Angeles Broadway 3

The eye is the organ that was entranced by film, that enduringly emanates the fascinations and scars that were embedded into it by film, and whose own movement of image-registration and projection – intimate with, but also essentially mismatched with, that of film – may involuntarily recoil from film's abandonment, and from the disintegration of cinematic space, with such force, like the convulsion that animated the hand of the ex-projectionist outside the Los Angeles Theater, as the human eye becomes engulfed by the digital, that it may undergo a profound transformation, engendering new visual forms that incorporate and revivify film's end.

The junction of Broadway and 7th Street in Los Angeles's Downtown forms the mid-point axis for the ruined cinemas of Broadway, just as it did for the immense human traffic of the area, during its zenith of the 1920s and '30s, and also through the war years, when those cinemas remained open all night to transmit newsreels of battles in the Pacific ocean and in Europe; the long-vanished tramways which brought Los Angeles's inhabitants to Broadway's attractions and department stores congregated around the junction to unload their passengers. At that junction, the State cinema was constructed in 1921 with foyers and marquees on both Broadway and 7th Street, and from outside the surviving foyer, that of Broadway, the entirety of the signs of the other eleven cinemas can be seized by the eye, which must contort its way through the turmoil of contemporary street signage, as though negotiating a labyrinthine film-narrative, in order to pinpoint those seminal cinematic traces.

All of the other cinemas of Broadway form initially barred, impenetrable spaces, that demand delicate negotiation or covert action to enter. The religious cultists at the open entrance to the State cinema, by contrast, adeptly employ multilingual temptations to entice the passers-by – often far-gone and acutely in need of salvation – into the grandiose interior of the 'Catedral de la Fe', in a new variant of the way in which, during that cinema's period of glory, smartly uniformed 'barkers' (eye-catching young men and women employed to vocally persuade wavering spectators to enter cinemas, by loudly extolling the film programme's attractions) previously channelled Broadway's transient population into that space, now mutated beyond film. But residual filmic hallucinations still hang suspended in the air, meshing with the religious visions of the hard-core cultists, each seated in isolation, interspersed with accidental spectators, across the auditorium's stalls, awaiting the beginning of the hourly services; unless closed in anticipation, their eyes stare at the vividly coloured planetary formations painted on the cinema's original asbestos fire-curtain, in front of which a pulpit now stands, while huge wooden crosses have been erected, close to ceiling-level, on either side of the screen. The cinema's infrastructure has not been permitted to lapse into disintegration, in its separation from film; the cultist proprietors maintain intact the perfect suspension of cinematic abandonment, and the crystal chandeliers above the balcony level appear oblivious to their new status, of illuminating religious rather than cinematic enflamings, as though the sensorial blurring of devotion that often induced cinema proprietors of the 1920s and '30s to advertise their buildings as 'cathedrals of film' had momentarily resolved itself in that space. Once the service starts, intermittent glossolalia convulsively erupts from the spectators, as though in anger, so that the former cinema emanates an unruly passion, like that animating all-night cult-movie seances, able to tear the spectators out of their seats in self-abandoned spasms. And at the heart of bliss, at the moment before the service's end, the incandescence of film-memory materializes in an ecstatic rush: memory without history, since film's history appears erased, and cinematic time may now head in any direction, forwards or backwards, or impale itself into the contemporary moment of its own disappearance.

Across Broadway, the prominent marquee of the Globe cinema features an illuminated exclamation of its name, and a metallic planet, like a vividly coloured eye overlooking the city, the oceans marked in blue, the continents in red; that ramshackle facade was

Globe cinema facade.

designed in 1945, to mark the cinema's new identity as a newsreel cinema, by S. Charles Lee, the legendary architect of Broadway's Los Angeles Theater and Tower cinema (and of many other spectacular cinemas in California, that determined cinema design worldwide), by then reduced to remodelling the surpassed designs of other architects after his own 1930s era of extravagant glory had evanesced. Behind Lee's facade, the cinema's original name from its construction in 1913 – the Morosco – is inscribed in austere letters on the building's stone surface. And below its own lettering, the Globe's marquee holds four fluorescent tubes of light, on either side of its planet, some of them operative, others blown, as though, like urban digital image-screens, half-heartedly advertising a void. Below those fluorescent tubes, a banner attached to the marquee's edge announces the contemporary occupant of the cinema's foyer: 'Teresa's Bridal and Tuxedo', so that the projected layers of time intersect intricately within that cinema's facade.

The bridalwear store occupied only the foyer, with the cinema's interior walled off behind it. But a barely marked doorway in the forbidding, urine-sodden alleyway that ran parallel to Broadway, behind the cinema, allowed entrance to the auditorium. In the twenty or so years following the cinema's closure in 1987, it fell into ruination; only bare fragments of its existence as a cinema – several lavish spectators' boxes and a marble staircase going nowhere – survived the gutting of the space, with the seating removed, the walls' sumptuous decoration excoriated, and the floor levelled, then concretized. The cinema's tenuous ownership, seemingly as undetermined as the building's future, enabled it to be hired by all-comers, over a period of several months, for haphazard events that always began late in the night, so that its status veered wildly. It covertly operated for a time as a Korean-run sex club, emitting a disparate form of sensory enflaming from that of the State cinema's hardcore religious frenzy across the street, and forming a literal embodiment, within that space, of the pornographic images that, preceding its closure, had been among its last filmic media, with live sex acts conducted for desultory audiences on small twin stages, sited in front of the now-vanished screen (at the club's alleyway entrance, a marker-penned sign, sellotaped to the aluminium door, announced 'absolutely no ins and outs' to its prospective entrants). Young performance artists and experimental filmmakers occasionally hired the bleak, echoing space for one-off, improvised events, and used it to project films at deviant vectors to that previously traversed, during its cinematic era, by the projector-beam. Another sex club then momentarily occupied the auditorium, with industrial extreme-noise cacophony shaking its cinematic traces, the pierced and tattooed participants driven towards orgasm by arrhythmic sonic delirium. After the alleyway entrance had been bolted shut for several months, the space re-opened, with its previous sex club apparitions erased, as a more conventional nightclub, though doomed from the start both by its suave patrons' unwillingness to negotiate the ill-lit alleyway's urine-pools, and by the negative inflections imparted to the clientele's dance-gestures by that awry space's residue of film, which appeared to imbue an intransigent charge of cancellation, and of cinematic death, into every gesture. Following that nightclub's abrupt closure, the Globe's auditorium returned, as though with relief, to its abandoned status and to its regime of suspended cinematic disintegration.

Film's Disintegration

At film's end, the disintegration of its medium and spaces are experienced pre-eminently by the eye, which must process the fundamental visual and corporeal transformations constituted by that terminal point, and discover ways to respond to it. But before those strategies can be developed – in the immediacy of the eye's separation from film, in advance of its habituation to the visual media and spatial configurations which supplant film – the eye must first experience film's end as an assault directed against it, and which may recall the intentions of experimental filmmakers of the late 1920s, such as Dziga Vertov and Luis Buñuel, to activate or attack the eye, in their attempts to forestall the spectatorial complacency which they associated with the rise of film-industrial genres and the sound-synchronisation of cinema, each of which subtracted from the spectator's active participatory role in film. The eye's forcible separation from film entails an interval of shock, prior to that habituation to film's loss, and film may appear still extant in that interval, as an afterburned retinal presence, but is now un-locatable, no longer tangibly there, so that human vision must construct a sequence of increasingly disordered and abandoned gestures within and through space, like the awry beams of a vio-lently shaken film-projector, in its search for filmic images.

When the eye is located in abandoned cinematic space, it may experience an unsettling disintegration similar to that provoked by film's loss, initially perceiving abandoned space as vertiginous, then as space for an active visual refiguring. If a cinema has been re-used for a purpose which has left its infrastructure essentially intact, poised in suspension, as with Broadway's State cinema, the eye is presented with a quandary of identification in which the conditions for film survive, but film and its history have been expunged, so that filmic memory itself must resurge in that space to contrarily mesh the space's contemporary re-use with its inerad-icable filmic aura. Whenever a cinema is subdivided into multiplex spaces, as often happened in the 1980s to large auditoria or to film-palaces in financial distress, its disintegration forms a literal spatial fragmentation, into lesser compartments, often pitched beyond recognition and identification. The forms of cinematic space's disintegration are explored in the film-installation work of the Austrian artist Martin Arnold, who extracts short sequences from Hollywood films, often genre films of the 1940s or '50s, and jarringly interrupts, repeats and recombines their elements; those sequences are projected in art-museum spaces conceived as darkened cinematic zones of fragmentation in which the spectator must immediately anticipate the utter loss of film's familiar, underpinning components (its duration, its narrative), and respond instead to compressed, askew filmic apparitions, from which unprecedented sensorial narratives, or hallucinatory intimations of film's cancelled presences, may emerge. For *Deanimated* (2002), exhibited at the Vienna Kunsthalle, Arnold used digital means to gradually erase the characters from the celluloid of the Hollywood horror film *The Invisible Ghost* (1941), until they entirely vanish, so that by the sequence's end, each shot, within which the camera's movements erratically search empty rooms, appears eerily voided of life, as though inhabited by exterminated filmic vision. In the art-museum installation space created for the projections of *Deanimated*, replicating aspects of the space inhabited by the original film's audience, the installation's visitor was intended to experience that compulsive effacing of film as entailing a corresponding disintegration of cinematic space.

Since film always entailed the generation of intense emotions, familiarly inciting outbreaks of mass weeping, sexual excitation, and a wide range of traumatic responses among its audiences, and also often demanded concentrated attention and memory-work to unravel labyrinthine plots such as those of mystery films, its end may be experienced by the spectator's eye as a profound relief. Film's supplantation by digital media and imageries which seek primarily to promote corporate formations, through a process of visual captivation, then become a source of bliss, as a release from film's relentless, century-long exigencies. Human vision often participates in an experience of elation and exhilaration whenever it witnesses the erasure of something to which it has been deeply attached, even though that erasure may also form a source of trauma. When film and its spaces are abandoned, that elation emerges from the realization that the power of an archaic presence has been arbitrarily returned to zero, wiped away, thereby enabling the generation of new visions, or new architectural forms, even if those visions and forms, involuntarily or not, may still be determined by residual traces or fragments of film. At film's end, the eye forms the vulnerable arena for the imprintation of the sensorial impacts – whether of elation or trauma, or of those impacts' multiple amalgams – which accompany that terminal moment, just as it did at the earlier, seminal filmic moments when filmmakers undertook experiments and active woundings on human vision.

Film's Eye-Experiments

The preoccupation of filmmakers with exerting particular impacts on their spectators' visual capacities, alongside the figuring of the eye itself as a presence within the filmic image, indicates the pivotal significance of human vision as simultaneously vulnerable to film's power, but also able to generate new imageries and to reconfigure itself, as it recoils from the upheavals or scarrings it receives from film, from cinema's origin to its end. Especially at moments of intensive mutation in the forms of film, as in the late 1920s, filmmakers experimented with intentional eye-assaults as a strategy to actively engage and transform their spectator's vision. Within cinematic space, an attack upon the eye, especially in experimental filmmaking, constitutes a break from the habitual regime of seduction or torpor experienced in the spectator's rapport with the screen, as well as from that spectator's luxuriant enclosure within such spaces as the lavish architectures of film-palaces. Film's end forms a contemporary, terminal variant of those experiments,

Man with a Movie
Camera, 1929.

in which the spectator's eye experiences its forcible severing from film as an elating, disorientating assault that intimates both an abrupt abandonment and a visual propulsion into the future.

At a time of social and visual upheaval, the Soviet filmmaker Dziga Vertov saw the expansive future forms of film as rendering the current human eye obsolete, and requiring an anatomical meshing of film-camera and eye; he proposed 'the use of the camera as a kino-eye, more perfect than the human eye, for the exploration of the chaos of visual phenomena that fills space'.[1] Especially in his films *Kino-Eye* (1924) and *Man with a Movie Camera* (1929), Vertov's enactment of an amalgam of camera-lens and eye takes place within the filmic image, as well as through its impact on the films' spectators, visually impelled into vertigo by the revelatory momentum of editing, and by the perpetual mobility of the camera itself. For Vertov, the active 'eye' of the camera lens expands to compensate for the deficits of the human eye, together with its subjugation within narrative-enslaved filmic forms and soporific cinematic spaces:

Our eye sees very poorly and very little – and so men conceived of the microscope in order to see invisible phenomena; and they discovered the telescope in order to see and
explore distant, unknown worlds. The movie camera was
invented in order to penetrate deeper into the visible
world, to explore and record visual phenomena, so that we
do not forget what happens and what the future must take
into account . . . Under the electric narcotic of the movie
theaters, the more or less starving proletariat, the jobless,
unclenched its iron fist and unwittingly submitted to the
corrupting influence of the masters' cinema.[2]

Vertov's project spans revolutionary and ocular forms, inciting a
surpassing of their current dimensions; his film-camera ascends
far above corporeal and urban space in Man with a Movie Camera, in
whose closing sequences he exceeds and assaults the eye with his
editing of rapid-fire images. That strategic attack upon the eye,
through the speed of editing, recurred in many 1960s experimental films, notably those of the Austrian filmmaker Kurt Kren,
with their one-frame cuts designed to precipitate visual disarray in
their spectators.

Even before Luis Buñuel sliced open the eye's surface with his
first film's initiating images in Un Chien Andalou, the Surrealist film-
theorist Antonin Artaud had already reflected on the necessity for
an intentional, directed ocular violence in film, designed to prise
open its spectator's vision; delineating his aims in writing the scenario for the first Surrealist film, The Seashell and the Clergyman
(1927), directed by Germaine Dulac, Artaud noted: 'We're involved
in researching a kind of film with purely visual situations, in which
the acts stem from an impact exerted for the eyes, taken, if I can
dare to say it, out of the substance of vision itself.'[3] Artaud excises
all narrational and sonic elements from his intended impact, which

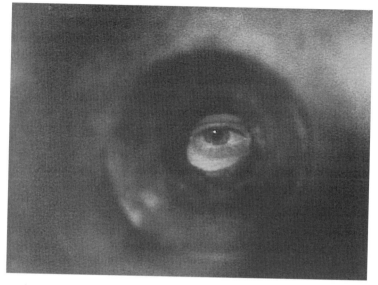

Un Chant d'Amour, 1950.

is simultaneously created 'for' the eye and also extracted from its own material, as though an over-obeisant eye needed to be ripped from its socket for its own good, to generate an irreplicable gestural moment of vision. In *The Seashell and the Clergyman* (whose film-premiere in Paris was marked by a riot), filmed eyes perpetually spin out of control, propelled from one hallucination to another, and the spectator's visual capacities experience a corresponding displacement, which Artaud intended to carry a charge of unleashed abandonment, both active and disruptive. Out of Artaud's theoretical film manifestoes, other strands of experimental cinema's explorations developed, such as those of Lettrist and Situationist film, in which cinematic space itself became attacked and overturned, along with its spectators' visions.

In experimental cinema of the mid-twentieth century, with its focus on far-reaching anatomical and visual transformations, the preoccupation with human vision comprises part of an attempt to puncture social confines and restrictions, and to allow sexual compulsions or liberatory acts to flow freely; but, in such films, the eye may also remain an acutely vulnerable medium which, at any moment, may itself be assaulted or perforated. In Jean Genet's film Un Chant d'Amour (1950), set in a prison of cells concealing the ritualistic sexual obsessions, and masturbatory dances and convulsions, of isolated male prisoners, the cells' spy-holes entice the guard in the corridor to pass from one barred door to another, enabling their contents to be viewed by the film's spectators; however, in the scenario for Genet's next film (planned, but then abandoned), The Penal Colony, the guard Marchetti, engaged in the same provocative insights as those of the guard in Un Chant d'Amour, has his eye fatally perforated by a needle wielded through the door's spy-hole by the watching prisoner inside. The filmic eye, within its visual image and its cinematic space, always possesses both deadly and seductive auras. But, in films concerned with the fascination with such assaults, an attack upon the eye may contrarily engender entirely new, unanticipated imageries, even when the assault appears to have terminally extinguished the capacity for vision; Gary Tarn's film Black Sun (2005) generates exploratory images, of urban blurs and landscapes in flux as a counterpart for its vocal narration by the French artist Hugues de Montalembert, who recounts how he was permanently blinded by a corrosive liquid thrown into his eyes by assailants, and how that total loss of vision precipitated his desire to travel worldwide, endlessly.

Unseen Films

An act of visual extinguishment, such as that of film's end, creates unseen films and unknown cinemas. Film's end implies a moment of the loss of sight, seemingly as irrevocable – in bringing down darkness on the filmic eye – as the violent originating act of *Black Sun*, but simultaneously holding aberrant pinpricks of light, like those of camera-obscura devices and pinhole cameras in the pre-history of cinema, which gradually amass to illuminate unprecedented imageries; residues of filmic memory may form an integral element of those imageries' instigation. Similarly, in entering the space of an abandoned cinema such as those of Los Angeles's Broadway, the initial darkness of the derelict auditorium may appear all-engulfing, permitting no possibility of exploration, but since such spaces are often perforated by, for example, ajar fire-doors at balcony level, beams of light progressively reveal the transformations undergone by cinematic space in its assaults by ruination, neglect and intentional damage, such as graffiti: transformations that negate the spatial possibility of filmic projection, but intimate the potential for new, sensorially excessive amalgams to materialize – such as the amalgam formulated by Dziga Vertov, between the eye, out-of-control speed, and the visual image – in those sensitized arenas for human vision.

Film's fade-out may be seen as the result of a prioritization of the digital over the filmic, as though those two visual media constituted a binary sequence from which the digital needed to be given precedence in order for its power to develop, and was prioritized for its aura of innovation and technological ubiquity over the century-old archaisms and incipient decrepitude of the filmic. During the era when the filmic and the digital still appeared as two autonomous entities, they were often perceived as an uneasily twinned pairing, like two mismatched eyes in the same face, in which the filmic eye had suffered a malfunction, or been subjected to an intentional assault, so that, as its vision diminished, the digital eye gradually 'corrected' that failing by strengthening itself, finally taking over the work of visual perception and image-generation in its entirety. At the extreme limit of the conflict between the

Andrei Rublev, 1966.

filmic and the digital, film's end may be seen as an intentional act of violent mutiny by the digital, to enhance the corporate imperatives and spatial expansions of the digital era: an act, then, of filmic blinding, with the aim of cancelling film's images and of voiding cinematic space.

In many films, the act of blinding often aims to impede the carrying-through of grandiose, visually oriented projects which must then find ways to mutate in order to achieve their realization in other forms. In Andrei Tarkovsky's film *Andrei Rublev* (1966), for example, a group of masons on their way to construct a mansion are blinded by the henchmen of a prince whose jealousy of the grandeur of what is to be created compels him to order the erasure of that mansion before it can even come into existence; the mansion will be unbuilt, but the monk-artist Andrei Rublev's apparent anguish at hearing of the act of blinding compels him to end a period of stasis in his artistic work and begin again, initially painting his icons with dirt. The filmic act of blinding may be self-directed, too, and still engender a compelling spectacle rather than the utter erasure of vision; in the Japanese filmmaker Toshio Matsumoto's *Funeral Parade of Roses* (1969), the transvestite Eddie decides to pierce his eyes with a carving-knife on learning that he has been engaged

*Funeral Parade of
Roses*, 1969.

in an incestuous relationship with his own father, but then reels in confusion into the crowded street outside his apartment, so that his loss of vision becomes a transfixing performative act for the audience of passers-by who surround and scrutinize him. Even at the heart of Hollywood's genres, the title of Douglas Sirk's 1954 melodrama of emotional and narrative excess around an accidental act of blinding, *Magnificent Obsession*, indicates that what appears to be the total extermination of vision always entails spectacular consequences.

The cultural experience of blindness in cinematic space was often one in which the companion of a sightless spectator would vocally narrate the ongoing events on screen to supplement the sonic bursts of dialogue and the distinctive tactile sensations of inhabiting that space, thereby constituting an intimate extension of the way in which, for early film-audiences worldwide, a narrator, standing alongside the screen, would give a vocal account of the silent film for the benefit of spectators not yet habituated to following filmic motion, or narrative forms, and for whom the film-images still resembled an illegible blur. At film's end, what lies 'beyond' film may form an experimental proposition of vision and language, like that generated in the mind of a sightless spectator required to amalgamate unseen, unknown images with sonic and vocal fragments, while corporeally positioned within the enveloping aura of cinematic space – and then to internally self-project the resultant multiply layered experience in order to conjure up the entity known as 'film'. Since digital images may only replicate corporate data, thereby forming part of those media which the filmmaker Werner Herzog, in the course of his appearance at the summit of the Tokyo Tower in Wim Wenders' film *Tokyo-ga* (1985), dismissed as being not 'adequate' for human vision, post-filmic spectators may feel impelled instead to envisage imageries which entail the same kinds of self-demanding experiences foreseen by 1920s eye-assailant filmmakers such as Vertov and Buñuel.

Fracture Points

The rapport between the 'magnificent obsession' of film and human vision was always a heated one, determined by fractures and misalignments between them; the tolerance of cinema audiences to conform to fixed parameters of filmic duration, narrative and montage always risked lapsing into a moment of abandonment in which the dissatisfied spectators would leave the cinema in exasperation at a 'bad' film. Equally, a film might compellingly transpierce and illuminate human vision in an inverse movement to that of filmic blinding, engendering fascination rather than extinguishment. Experimental cinema, from that of the Surrealists onwards, formed a laboratory for investigating the extreme variance of that interrelationship between the filmic image and the spectator's eye, extending from the notorious Surrealist cinema-going practice of repeatedly watching only a few seconds of a film before gratuitously abandoning the cinema and switching to another, to their theoretical preoccupation with film as an impact drawn from the eye, and inflicted upon the eye. At film's end, that rapport between film and human vision intensifies, since, if the eye still requires filmic images in order to vivify itself, it must now seize as much of their sensory and corporeal charge as it can before they entirely evanesce. The spectator's eye at film's end then ideally becomes a form of shutter, of the kind controlling the speed at which a film-camera records images, that has become jammed open and can no longer close (like the pupils of the delinquent film spectator Alex in Stanley Kubrick's A Clockwork Orange, 1971), out of filmic obsession, in order for human vision to fully incorporate last images.

In the opening moments of Blade Runner, between shots of Los Angeles's corporate towers expelling vertical bursts of flame, the image of a transfixed eye appears (that of Holden, the doomed blade-runner about to interrogate, and be maimed by, the replicant Leon, high up in the Tyrell Corporation building), and that panorama becomes imprinted into its transparent pupil. The image of the eye initiates the film, through that organ's absorbing of the maximal quantity of darkness, fire and light, the fragmented traces of which extend to the far perimeters of the iris; whatever transformations or mutations may occur across the film, including those oscillating around the boundary of the human, are encompassed in that moment. The spectator stares at the filmic eye; but as the images then move onwards from that seminal image, a fracture between film and eye gradually grows and magnifies, as the status of the authenticity of vision disintegrates, through the anxiety that what is seen is being perceived by replicants, and is therefore inaccessible and inassimilable to human eyes (as the replicant Roy asserts: 'I've seen things you people wouldn't believe'); the film's spectator, enduringly possessing the desire to envisage those unbelievable, denied 'things', then becomes pitched into a terrain of aberrant, impossible vision, conceivable only filmically.

Eyes are perpetually in extreme danger in Blade Runner: Tyrell dies through his eyes' perforation by Roy's fingertips, and Deckard

Blade Runner, 1982.

barely escapes a similar extermination at Leon's hands; ocular materials, together with their disintegration or fragmentation, form the core of the narrative and its mysteries. Deckard is able (through the intermediation of technology to magnify vision) to pinpoint a profoundly hidden human face within the initially illegible surface of Leon's photograph of his fellow replicant, Zhora. At the Tyrell Corporation, Deckard subjects the unknowing replicant Rachael to the 'Voight-Kampff' test which determines human-ness, and involves the placing of a screen-eye device on the table separating them. The screen visualizes an image of Rachael's eye in extreme close-up: an image which Deckard can view, but Rachael cannot. Before the test begins, Tyrell mockingly incants the responses whose transmission will indicate whether Rachael is human or not: 'fluctuation of the pupil, involuntary dilation of the iris'; for Tyrell, memory is the obsession which must be transmitted, even if it involves a terminal duplicity and fabrication. At the end of the test, during which the dimensions of Rachael's pupil have fluctuated erratically, in a strange mismatch with Deckard's professional expectations as he poses his statements for response, an image appears which forms the negation of the image at the film's opening, that encompassed Holden's intently watching eye. The Voight-Kampff device appears to extinguish itself independently of Deckard's intentions and actions, or else to have malfunctioned; the image of Rachael's eye vanishes, and the screen-eye turns to static, then wipes out into darkness. Within that mysterious narrative process of erasure, Deckard is able to deduce that Rachael is not human.

Throughout film's history, its imageries of human vision served to locate human and urban fracture-points, propelling the spectator's eye towards and into them, just as the inhabitation of abandoned cinemas, such as those of Los Angeles's Broadway, involves a process directing the eye into strata within which the seminal visions of film have gone awry, and in which an underpinning element of the city has collapsed; derelict or re-used cinematic space also tangibly transmits to the buildings surrounding it (many of them accordingly distressed or dilapidated) the loss of the pivotal aura of film. Many films, Blade Runner above all, comprise inexhaustible, all-engulfing archives of the manifestations and workings of the human eye, storing its gestures, impacts and assaults, its determinations of authenticity, together with the urban architectures which its forms inspire; implicit in such films – and explicit in Vertov's Man with a Movie Camera – is an exploration of the compulsive, uneasy rapport of interdependence between film and the eye, and of the potentially calamitous consequences of that rapport's cancellation through film's end.

Awry Visions

In the great film-palaces of the 1920s and '30s, such as the Los Angeles Theater and the equally grandiose Orpheum cinema on Los Angeles's Broadway, cinematic space often worked against itself to deflect the spectator's attention from the film; the interior of the cinema itself was intended to present such a multiplicity of attractions, and an engulfing sensorial environment in its own right, so that the act of film-projection could become almost a subsidiary spectacle for the more distracted members of the audience, to be absorbed in short bursts between periods devoted to the space's wide range of competing visual demands and physical luxuries. In some cinemas, as in the Los Angeles Theater, film-projection even became a spatially fragmented process, the images on the main screen simultaneously diverted into subterranean spaces in which socializing audiences, immersed in inhabitual architectural opulence, perceived those images tangentially, without the coherence of narrative. As the cinema-historian Maggie Valentine records:

The Los Angeles lounge . . . featured a prism designed by an engineer from the California Institute of Technology that projected the movie from the main screen in the auditorium to a small screen in the lounge. Each of these lounges was large enough to accommodate 450 persons . . . Opening off the ballroom were several ancillary rooms assigned to patrons' real and imaginary needs. One could use the smoking room; music room; nursery, complete with carousel, toys, and attendant; restaurant; and elaborate restrooms. The ladies' lounge in the Los Angeles was equipped with sixteen toilet stalls, each appointed in a different Italian marble. The make-up room contained chairs, tables, and mirrors framed in light bulbs, further enveloping a woman in her role of actress for the evening. For men, there was a shoeshine stand of pink Carrara marble.[4]

In the course of the great expansion of cinematic ambition which was at its height in the late 1920s, film-palaces still more architecturally extravagant than the Los Angeles Theater were constructed, pre-eminent among them the Roxy cinema in New York, built in 1927 and demolished in 1960, which possessed over 6,000 seats and a correspondingly magnified array of attractions, distractions and practical facilities, including a gymnasium, hairdressers, numerous shops and even a small hospital; one of the cinema's exits led directly into an adjoining hotel, so that wealthy patrons might almost literally live in the cinema (in an inverse way to that in which impoverished, otherwise-homeless people inhabited the never-closing cinemas of Los Angeles's Broadway during their terminal period of dilapidation). Such vast spaces as the Roxy were conceived to incorporate all of the visual enticements, luxuries and essential resources of entire cities, thereby literally constituting 'cinema-cities'. In such environments, the cinema inhabitant's vision far exceeded the parameters of filmic spectatorship, vertiginously searching for ever more intense sensations. During the destruction of the Roxy cinema in October 1960, the now-aged film star Gloria Swanson, one of whose films had been shown on the cinema's opening night over thirty years earlier, entered the demolition site in a black ball-gown and feather boa, and struck extravagant poses in the ruins for a photographer from *Life* magazine, poised in that ripped-open terrain of cinematic obsession and abandonment.

The human eye, in film, forms an aberrant medium of vision that rarely sees straight. The eye can appear to be the originating authority within a film, as with that of Holden in *Blade Runner*, but it may soon be propelled into a set of dizzying tangents and gestures which overturn that authority. In Hitchcock's *Vertigo* (1958), the eye seems to possess an omniscient power in the opening credit-sequence, which focuses on both eyes, then a single eye, of the duplicated character, Madeleine/Judy, who will plunge to her death twice in the course of the film; the film's title, and its director's name, even emerge outwards from within the eye's pupil, along with spiral shapes which intimate that the filmed eye, if it chose to, could expel not only the film *Vertigo*, but an infinite number of films impelled by the spatial and temporal obsession with spirals, such as the artist Robert Smithson's film *Spiral Jetty* (1970), of his vast earthwork-construction extending into Utah's Great Salt Lake. But even within that moment of the eye's omniscience, it is already distractedly veering, looking from side to side, before it eventually focuses on expelling its filmic content. Within *Vertigo*'s narrative, the eye's dubious authority also serves to configure and expose essential elements of time; in the sequence located in Muir Woods, to the north of San Francisco, Judy examines the cross-sectioned, exhibited trunk of a centuries-old sequoia tree, cut open and displayed like a dissected iris, and, in her doubly fraudulent persona of Madeleine impersonating the ghost-presence Carlotta, Judy is

Vertigo, 1958.

able to pinpoint, and articulate, the fragile temporal parameters of her life within the tree-trunk's strata: 'Somewhere here I was born, and here I died.'

At pivotal moments in *Vertigo*, the characters' eyes generate aberrant visions as they wildly search excessive space, like the eyes of a spectator-inhabitant of the luxurious film-palaces of Los Angeles's Broadway. As the detective Scottie desperately clings to the edge of a building's roof (as Deckard does in *Blade Runner*, before being saved by the replicant Roy), having fallen during his dangerous pursuit of a criminal, his eyes veer incessantly, upwards towards the policeman who is trying to save him, then abruptly downwards, in panic, into the alleyway below, as the policeman slips and plummets to his death. The filmic eye's gestures serve to chart death and terminal moments, but those gestures may become acutely disordered ones. The eyes of Judy, too, always look askew, tilting towards peripheral space, at awry tangents to their intended objective. In the sequence located in the stables adjacent to the San Juan Bautista mission, shortly before Judy ascends the mission's bell-tower (a tower which – as Chris Marker notes in his film *Sunless*, about his obsession with the visual memories of *Vertigo* – never actually existed, and had been conjured by Hitchcock) in order to simulate Madeleine's death, she is supposed to be intent on kissing Scottie; but her eyes suddenly veer away, in extreme variance to their presumed focal point, in order to stare in the opposite direction, towards the site of death. The eye, in films of visual compulsion such as *Vertigo*, constitutes a perverse presence which intersects with the experience at film's end, when the abandonment and ruination of cinemas generates a moment in which vision can no longer firmly focus on the tangible residues of film's existence, now destabilized and collapsing, and so must locate new ways to re-assemble film's traces; in its relationship with film, the eye forms a perpetually veering, probing organ, impelled to look beyond habitual boundaries.

Narratives of Film's Erasure

Any journey through a 'cinema-district' entails a distinctive narrative of its own, whether it is one in which the cinemas still exist in a state of abandonment, as in Los Angeles's Broadway, or else one in which the cinemas have been comprehensively demolished and appear to be erased in space, as with Tokyo's Asakusa district or San Francisco's Market Street; even in such spaces of apparent erasure, unforeseen traces subsist, often subject to radical transformation or re-use. In all cases, the narrative is a shattered one, in which the linearity of history, and of film history, has come unstuck, and abruptly veers backwards and forwards in time, just as Judy's mysterious eyes oscillate compulsively in *Vertigo*'s credit-sequence. At film's end, narrative becomes an endangered entity; it may now be consigned to an experience of its momentary apparitions, in the same way that the 1930s audiences of excessively luxurious film-palaces such as the Los Angeles Theater experienced narrative, in transit from space to space, beyond the auditorium, occasionally absorbing short bursts of narrative in between, and meshed with, an infinity of competing distractions. In its contemporary formation, the experience of narrative may also constitute one of incessant repetition, like that undergone by the homeless inhabitants of the Broadway cinemas at their low point of the 1970s and '80s, when derelict spectators literally lived in the never-closing cinemas, certainly oblivious to the rudimentary narratives of the films (often pornographic, or martial-arts films) being relentlessly projected, again and again, but still vulnerable to those narratives' gradual infiltration into vision and consciousness.

Many of the genres initiated by Hollywood and other film industries, especially in the 1930s to '50s, such as crime-thrillers, were conceived with the explicit intention that their narratives would be interchangeable and expendable, recognizably consisting of generic 'shorthand' forms to which audiences quickly became habituated. In that way a spectator focusing on a film for the entirety of its duration could experience a pleasure of fulfilled expectations, and of being able to assert, to fellow spectators, that they had known what was coming, that they had 'seen through' the film's narrative. Simply to consume and assimilate narrative may form an intense pleasure in its own right; as a result, enigmatic or demandingly multilayered films such as Vertigo were often badly received. Equally, that narrative predictability might render an audience restless, so that film's generic forms were frequently required to amend themselves and to incorporate new narrative permutations and variants in order to avoid the dissatisfaction of an audience that exited the cinema in oblivion, with no enduring memory of the film they had watched. From time to time, generic forms, such as the Western, having reached a point at which their audience had become exhausted by narrative repetition, would be withdrawn, and disappeared entirely, entering a cryogenic state for a period before re-emerging. In many ways a perpetually distracted audience, in such attraction-saturated cinematic spaces as the Los Angeles Theater, might be subject to a more compelling experience of filmic memory – in receiving a film's narrative fragmentarily, in instantaneous but concentrated bursts, and through tangents – than an audience exposed to the entire duration of a film's disposable narrative. The loss of all but essential instants of narrative could also constitute an intense spectatorial pleasure.

Experimental film often interrogated the ways in which the disruption or deletion of narrative could entail a different order of sensations for its spectators. Surrealist films of the 1920s such as those of Buñuel, Germaine Dulac and Man Ray adopted a wilful blurring of the fixed times and spaces of narrative, so that the intertitles, indicating the action's timeframe, inserted into films such as Un Chien Andalou, intentionally scrambled and undercut the spectator's hold on narrative in order to prioritize the impact of the film-image itself. In later decades experimental filmmakers preoccupied with issues of duration and the strategic erasing of narrative, such as Kurt Kren, used an editing approach designed not only to separate shots into one-frame cuts, but, at the extreme limit of narrative, to generate entire films made of a single shot or film-frame and imbued with calculated ephemerality, such as Kren's three-second-long No Film (1983), whose title intimates that, maximally devoid of narrative, a film either has no existence, or its existence has to be actively re-conceived from scratch by its spectator. Conversely, for Kren and other filmmakers concerned with the structures of film and its cinematic projection, such as Ken Jacobs and Stan Brakhage, the duration of the filmmaking process itself could extend into an almost limitless reflection on the implications of narrative, and the rapport between the film-image and the human eye. Many visual artists, too, Francis Bacon above all, experimented with retaining human figuration while suppressing all narrative elements from their work, entailing the intended elevation of an impact of sensation or memory, which might result from that erasure of narrative.

At film's end, the memory of filmic narrative can constitute a consoling presence, in the way that long-term prisoners, confined to cells, are often said to be able to visualize entire films across the same duration as the originals within their memories, and to re-play the narratives of those films as an antidote to an existence which may be one of unremitting repetition. Equally, film's ex-spectators may abruptly recall revelatory bursts or shards of narrative, of brief duration, in the same way that the audiences of 1930s film-palaces might remember the moments of film they had glimpsed between distractions, and which thereby became instilled with a particular, concentrated aura, able to traverse time and resurge at will. The pre-eminent contemporary, or future, form of narrative may be that transmitted by pervasive digital image-screens in urban environments, consisting of short, looped animations extolling corporate products or technology conglomerates, projected in relentless repetition, so that their narrative content gradually infiltrates their audiences' vision and consciousness, in the same way that the 1970s homeless inhabitants of Broadway's rundown, 24-hour cinemas assimilated the narratives of incessantly projected pornographic or martial arts films. In response to that over-exposure, the future human eye may desire more autonomous narrative forms, inflected by film's own momentary, fragmentary revelations.

Cinematic Austerity

Film's terminal disintegration removes all trace of the luxury once closely associated with cinematic space, engendering an austerity at extreme variance from the visual and corporeal lavishness originally instilled into the audience's experience of that space. Alongside the multiple distractions of such cinemas as the Los Angeles Theater, in which the spectator's eye was excessively 'spoilt for choice' as it transited between abundant sources of enticement or rapture, many cinemas of the 1920s and '30s aimed to fix their spectators' position within opulence, enabling those spectators then to scan in detail an extravagant environment that entirely engulfed their bodies. In the Kino Riga, for example, the luxurious rococo decor of the palatial waiting-rooms and auditorium implied that the spectator could be content inexhaustibly to explore the elaborate detail of the cinema's space, indefinitely, in stasis, almost without the need for any film to be projected; the sumptuous art deco Teatro Eden cinema, constructed in 1931 on Lisbon's Avenida da Liberdade, intimated explicitly that its audiences had entered a divine space from which there could be no advancement, and nothing further or more perfect to be experienced (that sense of occupying edenic space was perpetuated even in the moribund cinema's afterlife, when it was converted into deluxe apartments, so that an elite clientele could literally inhabit ex-cinematic space, a world away from the 1970s homeless inhabitants of the cinemas of Los Angeles's Broadway). That experience of an originating cinematic luxury was then augmented by the projection of films which often contained an equivalent extravagance in their set-designs.

The erasure of luxury entails an impact upon the eye which is one of withdrawal and subtraction; whereas Surrealist film theory envisioned a salutary attack upon the eye, and innumerable films figured the literal piercing of the eye's layers to deprive it of vision, the cancellation of cinematic luxury leaves the eye intact, but denudes and starves it. That deprivatory process may have a more widely corporeal origin, as in the spatial experience of ailing cinemas whose proprietors turn off the heating system and thereby reduce their spectators' body-temperature, but the eye remains the essential focus of the processes of denudation, at film's end, since the eye was rigorously habituated by film to search obsessively for visual plenitude and sensory gratification, to the point of aberrant excess. Film's austerity demands a contrary stripping-away to the essentials of the eye; in its rapport with film, the eye is no longer able to deploy its intricate range of ocular movements and gestures, which, during the zenith of such cinemas as those of Los Angeles's Broadway, comprised a distinctive cinematic language of the eye, developed by intensively scanning and exploring both lavish spaces and filmic images.

Many filmmakers presciently worked with materials that anticipated the raw remnants of film, once it is rendered into a condition of total denudation. Notably, Carl Theodor Dreyer and Robert Bresson intentionally reduced film's scope to an aesthetically concentrated form, to annul the spectacular power of representation, and magnify gestures through their rarity; a reduction of the possibilities of camera movement, and the use of extensive, static close-ups of the human face, as in Dreyer's *The Passion of Joan of Arc* (1928), manoeuvre the spectator into a position of immersal within minuscule transformations. In Japanese cinema, too, such as the films of Yasujiro Ozu, the concentration of film on particular sets of gestures, strategically stripped of all extraneous elements, and on narrative forms in which human figures move irresistibly towards their disappearance, impels the spectator's attention to work within tightly delineated spatial areas but with a rigorous, sustained focus. However, filmic austerity was also one in which a near-total lack of resources could perversely generate a corresponding excess, as in the works of impoverished cult filmmakers, such as Kenneth Anger's *Puce Moment* (1949) and John Waters' *Female Trouble* (1974), into which detached shards of Hollywood's opulent glory and aura were transplanted in a mutated, degraded form, so that the once-pervasive lavishness associated with the Hollywood industry only precariously survives after being subjected to a loving derision. In more acute responses to film-industrial power, insolvent experimental filmmakers, such as Kurt Kren and Jack Smith, working with stripped-down film fragments, infused their work with wry inflections of film's captivating luxury in order actively to interrogate it, or turn it to their own ends.

The promoters of the northernmost of Broadway's abandoned cinemas chose its name explicitly in order to impress upon its prospective audiences the gratuitous, infinite luxury they would experience once they passed under that name, emblazoned above its foyer, and entered the Million Dollar Theater. Those cinemas, in their overturning into dereliction, now constitute 'zero dollar', or even sub-zero, spaces, apparently frozen in suspension beyond monetary resuscitation (the estimated cost of restoring the gutted, scorched-earth interior of the Rialto cinema to its original state would be around fifteen million dollars). At film's end, as its observers register cinematic space's denudation, and the deliquescence of film's imageries into thin air, it works with reduced, bare materials whose austerity, in many ways, forms the antithesis of over-saturated, inflated digital-media environments; however, as with a resolutely austere form of filmmaking which intensively focuses its spectator's perceptions into narrow parameters, as in Dreyer's films – thereby directing that spectator to undertake inhabitual and demanding work, in order to reveal vital gestures or traces of the human body – the filmically denuded eye may also transform its forcible visual constriction into one of extreme invention, to unleash unprecedented imageries.

Filmic Combustions

Human vision, from the origins of film, was directed to exercise extreme attention within cinematic space because of the insistent danger of fire engulfing that space; projectionists and proprietors of cinemas needed to scan their spaces closely, since all early film-projectors risked overheating and bursting into flames, and the highly inflammable nitro-cellulose base of film-celluloid could also engender catastrophic acts of combustion, thereby establishing an intimate correspondence between the human eye, fire and film. The multiple incendiary events in the first years of film-projection, in confined spaces such as nickelodeons, together with highly mediated conflagrations in cinemas across subsequent decades, also created a spectatorial association between fire and film that uneasily existed beneath, or within, the more prevalent association between pleasure and film. Those large-scale cinematic incinerations could be either accidental or intentional, and took the form both of panic-stricken, corporeal rushes, and the literal engulfing by fire of cinemas' audiences. A mass flight from an accidental fire led to a suffocating crush at a children's matinee at the Glen Cinema in Paisley, Scotland, on 31 December 1929, after a just-projected film-reel ignited in its can in the cinema's projection-box, filling the auditorium with toxic smoke; at the Cinema Rex in Abadan, Iran, on 20 August 1978, a catastrophic, fast-moving fire was intentionally started, during the projection of a film, entailing the deaths of virtually the entire audience of between 400 and 500 spectators, immediately consumed by fire while still in their seats.

In ancient Greek philosophies of vision, the human eye itself may be the organ that illuminates what it sees, through the spatial

The Eye, 2002.

emanation of a form of ocular fire. The Pang Brothers' horror film *The Eye* (2002) depicts the hallucinations of fire experienced by a young musician named Angelica whose blindness has been rectified by a corneal transplant, conducted at a hospital in Hong Kong. As soon as the bandages are removed from her eyes, she begins to perceive blurred figments of bodies, and phantasmatic presences, generating a sense of terror, directed at her new eyes; something has evidently gone wrong in the transplantation of her new capacity for vision, and the film conjures an intricate meshing of visual and sonic malfunctions to intimate her hallucinations' disturbing sensory impact. Angelica awakens nightly to visions of a disaster entailing the mass combustion of human bodies. With a therapist's help, she gradually deduces that memory traces and warning flashes are being transmitted to her eyes by the corneas' previous proprietor, a young female 'seer' from rural Thailand who had committed suicide after her vocalized forebodings about an imminent fire at a sweat-shop factory were ignored. But even after Angelica travels to Thailand and placates the still-suicidal ghost whose corneal donation restored her vision, the new eyes continue to misfire. In a densely crowded avenue in Bangkok, Angelica experiences renewed, terrifying premonitions of a disaster by fire; stepping out from the bus in which she is travelling, she stares directly ahead, and the entire avenue abruptly explodes into the form of an oncoming fireball that carbonizes most of the avenue's occupants. Although the conflagration may ostensibly originate in the accidental ignition of a fuel-truck, the film presents Angelica's awry, ocular power as the intentional agent of that conflagration: film and the eye combine to unleash fire, which then acts back upon, and annuls, the eye, since flying glass-fragments pierce Angelica's retinas during the event, extinguishing her vision and returning her to a state of blindness.

In pathologies of the human eye, the neurological disorder known as 'visual extinction' indicates a condition, often caused by impairments of the right side of the brain, in which the eye is unable to focus on more than one object at any time; all entities beyond the singular become neglected and set aside, so that the multiple is foreclosed. If a filmic image were to constitute the unique visual focus of a patient experiencing the 'visual extinction' syndrome, that pathological attentiveness would carry both the obsessively determined devotion to film, experienced by its impassioned audiences for a century or more, and would also intimate

the acute watchfulness demanded, in cinematic space, of its proprietors and projectionists, to ensure that their spectators are not
engulfed in a conflagration by fire. That pathology also indicates
that even in an apparently terminal state of 'extinction', one image
may still survive in its attachment to its spectator's eye, even if that
image's future form, like that of film following its own erasure, may
be inflected by the process of disintegration which both created it
and made it 'unique'.

In determining the nature of human vision, Islamic theorists
across the ninth and tenth centuries, such as Al-Kindi and Ibn al-
Haytham, explored the profound mystery of whether the eye itself
illuminated what it saw, through the projection of fire-like rays of
light from the pupils, as in the extramission theory of vision, or,
alternatively, whether forms or bodies entered the eye in order to be
perceived, as in the intromission theory; Ibn al-Haytham (who also
first conceived of the pinhole camera) eventually argued that multiple rays of light, reflected from an object, illuminated it to the eye.
Those centuries-long enigmas form a counterpart to those investigated, in a more temporally intensified form, by film's pioneers of
the final decades of the nineteenth century, such as Donisthorpe,
Dickson and Le Prince, as they envisaged ways to project the film-
images they had recorded. For the Skladanowsky Brothers, in
Berlin, the film-camera could ideally be used both to record and to
project images, as though a filmic eye might be conceived that simultaneously registered and emitted its own images, thereby reducing
ocular theory to ashes. Film, in its volatile excess, always constitutes an aberration interposed within the forms of human vision,
thereby imbuing those forms with an inflection of film's integrally
incendiary presence. At film's end, its vital operations, such as its
intricate rapport with human vision, and the projection of its
images into cinematic space, enduringly carry that intractable aura
of mystery.

The Mystery of Film Projection 2

As with human visions that transmit themselves in dangerous rays of unruly fire, projection-boxes form supremely incendiary sites in cinematic space, and are often located at the origins of conflagrations – for example with the Glen Cinema fire of 1929 and innumerable other disasters – as though the smouldering film-reels causing the blazes were engaged in protest at being put back in their cans, and would be better struck to pieces with axes after unique acts of projection, as happened during the era when the recuperable mineral components of celluloid proved more valuable than the film-images it held. Among the abandoned cinemas of Los Angeles's Broadway, several of the ruined projection-boxes appeared spatially blown outwards, their charred walls seemingly impacted by a detonation from within, as though they had suffered a radical variant of 'visual extermination' syndrome in which not even a focus upon one resilient image could survive. I returned many times to the projection-box above the auditorium of the Los Angeles Theater, and the genial filmic die-hard, painstakingly engaged in overhauling its decrepit projection equipment for the cinema's yearly film-screening, offered to take me on his imminent filmic journey up the Californian coast, during the course of which he professionally maintained the equipment of the sparsely scattered cinemas which still employed celluloid, rather than digital, projection.

Midway between Los Angeles and San Francisco, in the town of San Luis Obispo, the Fremont cinema remained intact; its delicately arched tower, emblazoned with the cinema's name in vertical letters, rose above most other buildings in the town, and its ornate marquee prominently enticed prospective spectators. The pink-tinted cinema had been the luxurious last-gasp extravagance of S. Charles Lee, the architect who had begun his career in cinematic glory around the end of the 1920s with the Tower cinema and Los Angeles Theater in

Broadway, before being reduced to modifying the marquee of the adjacent Globe cinema in the postwar years. Commissioned in 1941 and originally promoted by its proprietors as the cinema 'of tomorrow', the Fremont's completion came six months after Pearl Harbor and the USA's entry into warfare, so that its construction was accelerated on borrowed time, since the government was intent on diverting all building materials into war-oriented construction; no new cinemas were then built during the remainder of the war. The walls and ceiling of the Fremont's interior had been vividly painted in art deco hallucinations of spirals and dancing figures, now faded; as with the Los Angeles Theater, damage from storm-seepage had generated a precarious terrain of intricate ceiling fractures. Since the cinema possessed no balcony, the aperture for the projector-beam, incised into the cork-panels of the cinema's rear wall, was located directly behind the stalls. The cinema's projectionist was assembling the reels of a colour-seeping, battered copy of David Lean's *Lawrence of Arabia*, and he displayed the same intensely focused, obsessional eyes as those of the Los Angeles Theater's filmic die-hard, as he recounted the genealogy of the cinema's gradual disintegration; the original screen had been so badly assailed in the delirious uproar of 1970s cult-film screenings that its use had been abandoned, and a new screen sited ten feet forwards, bringing the audience into intimate proximity with the film-images. The Fremont still attracted a devoted clientele, though a new cinema had been built nearby that embodied California's ecological preoccupations: the world's first solar-powered cinema, its roof crowded with large solar panels, as though, if any excess energy were generated beyond that required to drive the projector into action, it could be channelled directly into the spectators' eyes to unleash fire-impelled filmic visions in blinding incandescence.

Further north along the coast, the lavish solar apparition of Hearst Castle appeared, surmounting hills to the east of the Pacific

coast highway; profligately concocted from fragments of obsolete
European palaces and cathedrals, that lavish castle had attracted
innumerable film stars from Hollywood, intent on ingratiating
themselves with its proprietor, the all-powerful media tycoon
William Randolph Hearst. The castle possessed a small cinema on
its ground floor: as opulent, in its concentrated architectural form,
as those of Los Angeles's Broadway, the walls panelled in scarlet
damask and lined with gold-plated caryatids. That space formed
part of the distinctive lineage of private cinemas located in the
residences of entrepreneurs and figures of power, extending from
Hugh Hefner to Joseph Stalin, and used for ostentatious, late-night
screenings for elite guests. Hearst's cinema had been constructed
at the same moment as the Los Angeles Theater, and the Hearst
Castle cinema's most assiduous film star occupant had been
Charlie Chaplin, also present at the Los Angeles Theater's opening,
with its premiere of his film City Lights, in 1931. At eleven each
evening, Hearst's guests had assembled in the cinema for the
screening of new films that had not yet been released for public
consumption. The cinema was meticulously preserved, its perpetual
suspension emanating an aura of extreme abandonment, broken
intermittently by tourist-groups who stayed for several seconds to
watch a film-loop containing handheld sequences shot in the
grounds of the castle, showing its transient film star inhabitants,
playing tennis or gesturing and joking with one another, their faces
seemingly illuminated by elation at being guests of Hearst's prestigious eden. The cinema's elderly projectionist, confined in his duties
to the endless projection of that one unique film, appeared correspondingly elated by his experience of sheer repetition, as though
one film alone sufficed. In the early 1930s the film-footage shot of
Hearst's guests had been immediately developed on the spot, then
projected to those same guests in advance of each evening's main
screening. The near-simultaneity of that recording and projection

of images evoked both the experiment envisioned at film's origins by the Skladanowsky Brothers, of creating a device able both to register and emit film-images, and also the project that had preoccupied the Soviet filmmaker Alexander Medvedkin at that same moment of the early 1930s, of travelling incessantly by train with his collaborators, around a country haunted by famine and persecution, shooting sequences of the activities of impoverished peasant communities during the day, then developing the footage in order to project it, in the evening, to the same peasants, who had never seen film-images before, and often appeared stupefied and fearful, as though they were watching images of the dead. In the Hearst Castle's phantasmatic cinema-space – in which, as with the abandoned cinemas of Broadway, time wildly veered backwards and forwards, at film's end – a contemporary film-screening might be envisaged in which Hearst's re-animated, early 1930s film star guests could focus on ghostly, gesturing images of their now-evanesced, long-dead bodies, thereby engendering an unprecedented moment of self-startling, like that experienced by Medvedkin's film-denuded peasant audiences, as they tried to recognize images of their own bodies, and instead perceived only filmic death.

To the north of San Francisco, in the Russian River valley, the final cinema requiring urgent repairs to its projection-equipment, the Rio, formed the antithesis of the splendours of the Hearst Castle cinema: an extraordinary construction of rust-coloured corrugated iron, overlayered with a ragged patchwork of additional strips where the originals had come unstuck or worn through, and clawed open at one end, as though a vast rainwater drum had been sliced in half and haphazardly abandoned on its side, in a rural, forested landscape. As with the Fremont cinema in San Luis Obispo, the cinema's marquee featured a sign extending vertically, but, in contrast to the attention-seizing pinnacle of the Fremont's ornate sign, curtailed to only three letters: 'Rio'. That cinema appeared to have been conceived

Rio cinema.

as an act of derision for the very idea of 'cinematic architecture', forming seminal filmic debris at the edge of the Russian River. Across that river, along a narrow road named the 'Bohemian Highway', a private estate was located, hidden by dense barriers of sequoias, where a group of the USA's most powerful figures – former presidents, banking executives, media-conglomerate tycoons, known as the 'masters of the world' – notoriously held an arcane meeting, each July, in a strange mixture of homoerotic horseplay and profound deliberation, in order to determine the global future. The Rio cinema stood its ground at the Bohemian Highway's southernmost end, as though negating those global projects, through the now precarious, but integrally incendiary, medium of film. The cinema's projection-equipment appeared to possess the same last-ditch, disintegrating status as its architectural form, and its proprietor and projectionist evidently sustained that cinema's existence through an obsessional effort of will. Without that tenacious work of vision, poised a moment before cinematic abandonment, the vital entity of filmic obsession itself may be subject to a terminal fall into withdrawal – though that moment of vanishing, in itself, can precipitate unforeseen transformations, and resuscitated images.

PART 4

FILM AND FILM'S END: RESUSCITATED IMAGES

Los Angeles Broadway 4

The residual cinemas of the southernmost section of Broadway are visible from underneath the ramshackle marquee of the Globe cinema, occasionally illuminated by its proprietors, in order to entice a clientele into the bridalwear store now occupying its foyer, as though the omniscient planetary eye that surmounts that marquee, designed by S. Charles Lee in 1945, were still vivified by the phantasmatic presence of film inhabiting the dereliction of the cinema's nightclub-decor interior, and now wanted to see even further, all the way, until film's end is reached. Directly across 9th Street from the Globe cinema, the pristine side-facade of the Tower cinema is embedded, below its roof-level, with a sequence of vast panels, as large as digital image-screens, that once announced its filmic content, and also served as immense advertising surfaces for long-disappeared urban attractions; beginning from the cinema's rear with a panel still legible and announcing 'open all night', the shape of that sequence of panels appears as a celluloid strip, stretched horizontally, within which all content has eroded, disintegrating as calamitously as the film-images scrutinized in Bill Morrison's film *Decasia*. The wearing-away of the panels' content reveals previous layers of image and text, so that disparate announcements exist simultaneously, each now equivalently erased. A vitally illegible

Tower cinema facade (fragment).

language is projected from that facade, last updated during the era when the cinema incessantly showed newsreels of warfare and crisis, and frozen in that urgency, suspended in abandonment. The facade's intricate terracotta ornamentation forms frames for those panels in order to magnify still further their exclamations, but the panels' images and lettering have terminally blackened into indecipherability, occasional fragments still seizable, but finally remaining mysterious.

On the far side of the Tower, the elongated marquee of the Rialto cinema (the longest on Broadway, added in the 1930s to the cinema's facade, itself constructed in 1917) bears inscriptions in Spanish from downmarket clothing companies that once ephemerally used its interior, before allowing that cinema to become a profound zone of decades-long dereliction. In its extreme neglect, the Rialto forms the supremely abandoned space among Broadway's cinemas, its silent interior wrecked, strewn with inexplicable debris, the walls and ceiling excoriated, their original surfaces removed, so that only a tenuous network of wooden pediments and skeletal roof-girders supports that dangerously unstable space. Entering the cinema, through a door that had been locked for so long that the bolt had rusted, entails the experience of entering a vast tomb structure, like that of a Chinese emperor. Once the exterior door has closed again, the only illumination, through the thick dust hanging in the tainted air, is from a single, green-tinted lightbulb. The cinema's ground-level forms a scorched-earth terrain; most of the seating-space has been levelled and replaced by a terminal moraine of infinitely mixed debris, but at the rear of the cinema, a precarious section of the raked seating remains extant, accessible by a stairway suspended in space, so that ascending to the site of the blown-apart projection-box constitutes a perilous climb over a disintegrating structure. A few 1970s postcards showing children and female dancers, along with faded-out film-delivery schedules, are still pinned to the projection-box's collapsed walls. The nearby emergency exit is barriered from the inside against potential intruders, but an outburst of graffiti indicates that it was once breached, a decade or more ago, before being securely sealed. Wrenched-out electrical wires hang in the air, wildly askew, and the split-open walls leak their asbestos interiors. At the other end of the cinema, only the upper edge of the screen remains in place, jaggedly ripped, the remainder long gone, so that what survives for its illumination by film resembles serrated mountain-peaks, like those of Japan's Mount Nokogiriyama or Catalonia's Montserrat.

The inhabitation of that cinematic space is that of film's living end, which appears tenaciously suspended, and ineradicable: an endless end, for the entity of film. In the 1980s the Japanese photographer Ryuji Miyamoto recorded images of the demolition of redundant cinemas worldwide, photographing sequences of the once-grandiose interiors of those cinemas as they vanished into thin air. His images of cinematic space explicitly possessed an origin and a conclusion; as the art-historian Mark Holborn notes: 'They were captioned with the original date of the completion of the building, the name of the architect and the date of Miyamoto's own photograph. The passage of time from creation to destruction is stated.'[1] By contrast, the cinemas of Broadway elude destruction, poised in a perpetual abandonment which also constitutes a perverse endurance, and creates a crucial aperture, through film's essential aberrance, for resuscitated images. Once the exit-door of the Rialto cinema is reopened, midday sunlight floods into the space, revealing, with greater intensity, its aura of immense, raw neglect. At the same time, the contaminated air from that entombed space rushes out, through the ajar crack, into the present moment, entering the megalopolis of Los Angeles, as though carrying in concentrated form a vital, deadly virus, of film's survival, to the population outside.

At Broadway's southernmost extremity, the final apparition of that avenue's twelve extraordinary cinemas, the flamboyant United Artists Theater, forms a terminal exclamation-mark to that sequence, extravagantly surmounted by a bogus cathedral-tower; it was built in 1927, nine years after the Million Dollar Theater, at the other extremity of Broadway. The sequence of cinemas becomes extinguished as the avenue itself begins to deteriorate, from the point where the United Artists cinema stands; the dense activity and gestures of Mexican and El Salvadorian traders, and their clientele, abruptly evanesce, and the avenue mutates into a near-deserted, lost road, heading south towards the Watts Towers, occasionally traversed by homeless people with shopping-trolleys, in an urban void. As with the State cinema, the United Artists became the domain of a religious cult, once its filmic audiences had abandoned it; together with its architectural design, the cinema's revised name – the 'Los Angeles University Cathedral' – explicitly links its space to the 1920s concept of luxuriously protective 'cathedrals of film', promoted by the original proprietors of Broadway's cinemas. While the State's new proprietors actively entice passers-by inside, the United Artists cinema's opulent interior, partly modelled on the Gothic cathedral of Segovia (though also incorporating murals lauding the film stars and directors, including Chaplin and D. W. Griffith, who assembled to finance its construction), forms a more secretive space, devoted to research into biblical scholarship. It is accessible only to spectators with a real or feigned interest in its particular ethos and collection of religious artefacts, assembled by the legendary television evangelist Pastor Gene Scott, whose maniacal fundraising technique was the subject of Werner Herzog's film *God's Angry Man* (1980), and who bought the cinema outright in 2002, bequeathing it on his death to his widow, Pastor Melissa Scott, whose own multilingual explorations into biblical minutiae, performed to rapt audiences from a stage in front of the original site of the cinema's screen, are transmitted nightly in the Los Angeles area on cable television.

From the entrance of the United Artists Theater, the seminal traces of cinematic dereliction extend intermittently all the way back up to the Million Dollar Theater, in the marquees, signs and facades that insurge into the avenue. Beyond those marquees, the cinemas' interiors hold their volatile charge of abandonment, and of memory and obsession, held in suspension, but primed to be unleashed, across space and time, within the ongoing transformations and mutations of visual forms, for which film remains a uniquely ineradicable, haunting presence. Far above those cinemas' traces, the amassed corporate towers of Los Angeles extend vertically, several avenues to the west, cohered by their array of vast digital image-screens.

Filmic Conjurations

Such an abrupt shift between the abandoned cinemas of Los
Angeles's Broadway and the immense corporate screens that constellate the towers of the adjacent financial district, relentlessly
transmitting an exterior eruption of images, initially appears an
irresoluble one. But the visual dynamics of the filmic and the digital also constitute an integrally meshed arrangement, even when it
appears that film's status has been rendered into that of the subordinated partner within a volatile coalition, conceived in order for the
digital to extract from film its vital impacts, auras and architectures,
before eventually discarding its blood-drained husk. The spatial
and temporal disordering projected from Broadway's abandoned
cinemas intimates that contemporary visual forms, holding unstable charges of memory and residual filmic obsessions, comprise a
far more capricious arrangement than one in which film, after a
linear historical interval, is covertly 'disappeared' by the digital. At
film's end, time itself may veer from a point of redundancy to one
of seminal origination, as with the immense panels on the facade of
the Tower cinema, designed for the prominent display of image
and text, whose grandiose illegibility itself carries an intensive

Nosferatu, 1922.

visual impact, as powerful as that of the digital image-screens whose rapidly replaced content, similarly seizable only for a moment, before its evanescence, entails a parallel experience of illegibility, as though those screens' purpose was solely to cite the disintegrated hoardings of abandoned cinemas.

In film, there is always an urgent need to look behind you. In horror films, characters who fail to turn and glance over their shoulder, often misinterpreting the horrified, warning eyes of the friend they are facing, thereby neglect the deadly, weapon-wielding figure directly behind them, and suffer imminent erasure. In many films, the threatening figure forms a strangely beguiling one, as with the vampire Count Orlok in F. W. Murnau's *Nosferatu* (1922), who inhabits zones which interconnect life and death, subjugation and domination. Even though that outlandish figure exudes a pestilential or viral aura, like that threatening to escape from the tomb-like interior of the Rialto cinema in Broadway, he remains a focus of empathy, caught in the suspension of death, but infinitely undead and unendable, like film itself, and prone to all-consuming obsessions (notably with images, such as Hutter's photograph of Ellen): obsessions shared by film's spectators. Throughout its history, film's narratives, across all of its genres, conjured resuscitatory comebacks in which characters thought to have been exterminated, or consigned to an inescapable elsewhere, suddenly re-emerge, often materializing in a radically altered form. Any definitive barrier, even that of death in horror films, is filmically permeable. Film's history and future carry that same capacity to endlessly mutate; looked back upon, film is always shifting, and the act of envisioning film's future entails its transformatory amalgamation with new visual forms.

Film's impossible comebacks, in which a figure or entity believed erased can elude that visual annulling to become present in the film once again, often constituted a strategic event necessary for narrative development, in which that re-apparition, however improbable or unforeseen it might initially appear to its spectators, could, after a moment's resistance, be accepted, and cohered within their perception of the film. The abrupt return of an irrevocably lost entity invariably carries emotional resonances, as in Vincente Minnelli's film Brigadoon (1954), in which a mythical Scottish village, marooned several centuries in the past and accidentally reactivated by the intrusion of American tourists, appears to have become definitively lost once again, before finally re-materializing through the intervention of a character's obsessional desire. In Brigadoon, the resuscitation of the lost village forms a pivotal, redemptive event (the film would collapse in despair, for its spectators, if it did not occur), but that fracturing of time constitutes a gratuitous, impossible conjuring, as well as an essential narrative component, to be forcibly integrated into its spectators' perception, and sutured there as much by an engulfing musical soundtrack as through the work of images. The filmic re-apparition of what has vanished requires an element of outright sensorial caprice.

Film's pioneers of the 1890s worked closely with that sense of caprice and impossibility, partly since many of them believed that they were inventing a tenuous, ephemeral medium, rather than creating frameworks that would eventually stultify into fixed narrative forms. The conjuration of impossible filmic events, whose impact for their spectators depended upon the astonishing resurgence of such entities as vanished bodies, decapitated heads and missing anatomical components, is prominent throughout the work of magician-tricksters such as Georges Méliès and the Skladanowsky Brothers; since their films possessed a relatively brief duration, and formed part of a visual medium that itself appeared transient, their disappearance-tricks and re-apparitions could be manipulated with a maximal imaginative freedom and capriciousness. With the instigation of film-industrial genres, such as the musical melodrama

genre within which *Brigadoon* emerged, those impossible phenomena then needed to be integrated within narrative, as events which
justified themselves, by securing their characters' futures. But at
film's end, once narrative has mutated back into concertinaed,
mysterious forms of extreme brevity, such as those animated from
digital image-screens, its previous demands and justifications
abruptly go up in smoke in order to resurge in a new form, as with
Méliès' adept conjurations of vanished and resuscitated objects, at
the origins of film. Beyond its erasure, film transforms itself.

The Filmed Image-Screen

Image-screens, such as those of Los Angeles's financial district,
adjacent to the abandoned cinemas of Broadway, may now appear
hauntedly inhabited by the conjured images of film's trickster-
pioneers, as though those pioneers, such as the Skladanowsky
Brothers, had themselves feigned their disappearance (perversely
withdrawing from filmmaking and film-exhibition at the very
moment, in 1897, when the medium was rapidly escalating in popu-
larity) in order abruptly to reappear, with a revelatory narrative
closure, at a pivotal moment in film's history: its end, or its meshing
with the digital. The loops and sequences projected from image-
screens, designed for excessive visual impact within a maximally
curtailed duration, and primed for rapid oblivion, interconnect with
the conception of film, in work such as that of the Skladanowsky
Brothers, at its origins, as a project of beguiling evanescence; the
pre-eminence of digitally animated elements, within the content of
contemporary image-screens, also intimately resonates with the
adroit manipulations of human movement that attracted both
film's pioneers of the 1890s and also the experimental filmmakers
of the 1920s, such as Vertov. Experimental film, and Vertov's above
all, was also one in which film intersected with such media of visual

display as hoardings, billboards, vast political slogans and advertising panels, through the obsessive filming of those displays: media which prefigure digital image-screens. Especially in East Asian cinema, such as that of Wong Kar-Wai and Tsai Ming-Liang, the desire remains persistent to deploy the medium of film to scan and explore such prominent media of display as digital image-screens, as though activated by the need to interpose film's presence upon such screens, in reaction to the usurping by the digital of film.

Film's exploratory infiltration of image-screens unsettles their habitual corporate content – in the form of sequences lauding particular products or corporations – which itself possesses only a tenuous, surface-depth hold, secured by a provisional amassing of indifferent pixels, before their replacement. The visual collision of film and image-screens may disrupt the status of those screens as corporate power devices, and transmutate them into prescient image formations with close connections to the historical strata of film and its cinematic spaces, such as the overlayered display-panels of the Tower cinema's facade. In *Blade Runner*, notoriously inspired by the image-screens of the Shinjuku and Shibuya districts of Tokyo, the replicant Roy's terminal, filmically imbued statement to Deckard on the nature of memory and death is delivered against the enveloping background of an image-screen which simultaneously illuminates his body, as he delivers his last words, and also

Blade Runner, 1982.

Tokyo image-screens.

advertises the Japanese TDK Corporation, whose motto instructs its workers that: 'Performing power is born by confronting contradiction and overcoming it'.[2] Film and the digital constitute a vital contradiction within which visual power is at stake, and while the digital may overcome film through its strategies of pervasive dominance, film possesses the trickster-capacity to wryly undercut the digital, and infiltrate into it the deeply aberrant, memory-incised nature of its own projections.

Film can scan and interrogate the forms of digital image-screens, as a sensitized process originating in its previous explorations of hoardings, posters and neon billboards, but it may also, on occasion, penetrate the image-screen itself, and momentarily jettison that screen's corporate content, allowing spectators an insight into the potential for seminal, irreversible events, generated by confrontations between the filmic and the digital. In 2003 the Sony Corporation in Tokyo allowed the entirety of the immense image-screens affixed to corporate towers around the Shibuya intersection – the megalopolis's most densely occupied axis, inhabited by figures in transit on foot between the district's railway station and its department stores – to be infiltrated for several minutes by an experimental film shot, on Super-8 film-stock, in 1973, documenting

Bangkok image-screen.

a performance-art event undertaken at a moment of acute social tension in Japan. Although the Shibuya intersection's transitory inhabitants maintain a habitual obliviousness to the corporate imageries (lauding the range of Sony products) incessantly transmitted from those image-surfaces, the abrupt insurgence, within those screens, after a transitional moment of darkness, of a profoundly disparate visual content, and its multiple projection, led them to stop in their tracks, and engage in a momentary spectatorial astonishment, at the voiding of corporate imagery and the 'comeback' of film, in an experimental form, as though that intervention signalled the end of the digital, rather than film's end.

Image-screens, notably in East Asia, may also intimate a self-awareness of the grandiose frailty and potential malfunction of their corporate power (perpetually subject to economic meltdown, and to all-engulfing digital crashes) that remains absent from the Los Angeles financial zone's image-screens, which tower over Broadway's abandoned cinemas. At the Siam Square intersection of Bangkok, a vast image-screen advertising a global positioning system momentarily displayed an animation inciting its gridlocked spectators to 'take a look', and featured a succession of wildly pivoting eyes, together with the slogan 'irresistible media power'; the eyes are strangely suspended in space, disembodied, as though constituting abandoned images. The concentrational foreclosure of resistance to media power annuls all possibility of exploratory human movement, and of ocular experimentation, thereby negating the act of vision itself. At such a moment of precarious mutation within the nature of the visual, all image-screens are rendered open to their future overturning, into multidimensional, transformational media of vision, entailing a vital alliance between film's memory and the human eye.

Manias of the Human Eye

In East Asia, film has become terminally subsumed into other media forms, and into contemporary digital cultures, far more intensively than in Los Angeles's enduringly film-scarred avenues. Film's end often appears a clear-cut process in East Asia, as the tangible evidence of its memory vanishes (the riotous, multi-thousand-seating cinemas of Hong Kong, Macau and Bangkok, constructed in the 1950s, and designed, like New York's Roxy cinema, to constitute autonomous 'cinema-cities' in their own right, are gone without trace). Simultaneously, though, film's residual presence remains implicated within East Asian media, notably in the form of filmically propelled manias of the human eye. The digital image-screen of the Siam Square intersection, with its emphasis on the eye as the organ that unfailingly locates, and then incorporates, 'irresistible media power' – in a process that directly resonates with the film-spectator's desire to absorb an essential content, via the eye – intimates that the eye's role constitutes the pre-eminent one, which annuls or dismisses all other roles. Even that image-screen's textual assertion of 'media power' is consigned to a peripheral, lower corner, as though the screen's aim were not, after all, to impose a totalitar-ian media-power precluding all resistance, but instead to conceive of a form of power inciting a vertiginous sensory fall, like that pro-pelling a spectator into the domain of the provocatively enticing eyes of film stars, or the grandiose luxury of cinema-palaces: a fall which cannot be resisted, since it affords too deep and disorientat-ing a sensorial ecstasy for whoever abandons themselves to those filmic powers.

East Asian manias of the human eye also resonate with the obsessions of Dziga Vertov, in his *Kino-Eye* and *Man with a Movie Camera* film-projects of the 1920s, instigated for the development of an omniscient eye able to scan and record every last nuance of life and its traces, as though the eye were the only organ with the capacity to assemble a comprehensive visual archive of life, at a moment of revolutionary transition such as that of the Soviet Union's early years. The textual, by contrast, would be unable to seize the astonishing transformations of gestures, encounters, alliances and refusals whose uniquely sensitized archival space was to be that of the cinema, into whose arena all of the images amassed in *Man with a Movie Camera* are finally delivered, at the film's end, for projection to an audience of attentive spectators. In contemporary East Asian visual environments, that process of a frantic, near-infinite life-archiving, in the obsessional collection of images, remains a compulsive, film-incited project, embodied in the mani-cally swivelling eyes of the Siam Square intersection's image-screen, even though the resulting, wildly excessive archive of untold billions of digital images may well become redundant, and immediately evanesce, at the very moment of their capture.

The pre-eminence of the eye, as the instrument for direct contact with its often-excessive or threatening urban environment, is revealingly marked in all contemporary East Asian visual media. Even when the eye's movements misfire and provoke calamities, as in the Pang Brothers' film of conflagratory devastation sparked by haunted visions in Bangkok, *The Eye*, it remains the organ that is solely assigned the work of gathering reliable indicators of its environment, just as film's images, in its newsreel era during warfare, served to verify and confirm events, for spectators otherwise denuded of visual data. In predominantly digitized contemporary environments, in which the status and future forms of the corporeal appear unsettled, the eye in itself now frequently constitutes a corporeal as well as visual entity that supersedes the remainder of the body to become its sole-surviving outlet-point for the transmission of physical information, memories and desires to the outside world, while simultaneously forming the unique aperture for the absorbing of all external, incoming stimuli, thereby operating like the alarmed, disembodied eye of Judy/Madeleine in the opening credit-sequence of Hitchcock's *Vertigo*, which both emits and also lets in the film's vital data, becoming a 'story' in its own right. In its pre-eminent status within East Asian visual environments, the eye also takes on a filmically inflected role as the origin for the reinvention and adaptation of the contents of whatever it projects and absorbs, in a parallel process to the work of cinema-spectators who habitually sieved and reconfigured a film during its projection, in order for its contents to intimately gel with their own preoccupations.

Sexual desire within East Asian media environments is often focused on the human eye itself, whose flesh, movements and gestures become a primary source of fascination, so that the eye assumes the role of a uniquely sexualized organ in its own right, once other sexual organs, caught in the digital era's corporeal transmutations, may no longer form reliable indicators of desire. The eye may initially mesh with those other organs (a process prefigured in the work of Surrealist artists of the 1920s and '30s, such as Hans Bellmer, and also in Georges Bataille's depictions of disembodied eyes inserted into sexual organs, in his novel The Story of the Eye, 1928), or it may finally supplant those organs to become the seminal agent of sexual compulsion, and for the formulation of new visions of desire, transmitted multiply and in excess from East Asia's image-screens – in a form historically anticipated by film audiences' experience of a fixation with vastly beguiling, sexually imbued eyes, viewed in extreme close-up images, within opulently engulfing cinemas such as those of Los Angeles's Broadway. Film remains a profoundly embedded presence within the human eye, whose role now expands in irresistible power, beyond film, to inhabit new sensorial and spatial domains.

Cinematic Test-Zones

The space of abandoned cinemas, together with that space's posthumous transformations and multiple re-usages, as in Los Angeles's Broadway, indicates the capacity of human vision for its exploratory expansion, once it has been propelled beyond film. In that sense, Broadway's abandoned cinemas – in their divergent variants, from the infinite dereliction of the Rialto cinema to the frozen suspension of the Los Angeles Theater, all of them enduringly inhabited by filmic obsessions – together constitute a kind of test-zone for the invention of new entities and imageries. Such cinemas are often cordoned off and hidden from their surrounding environment, in a parallel way to that in which tracts of desert, in California and Nevada, are conjured out of existence to form militarized sites for the covert formulation of innovations in weapons technology. The re-usage of Broadway's cinemas – their auditoria densely packed with cases containing plasma-televisions, or else occupied by frenzied nightclub and church clienteles – then appears less as a random, improvised process, and to indicate instead an intentional strategy to create experimental arenas for the initiation of unforeseen media by placing film's incendiary remnants in close contact with digital technology, or with human figures in a state of unrestrained sensory uproar, in order to harness the unique fusions generated by those mutant amalgams of film with the digital, of film with the human body.

The atmosphere of the abandoned cinemas of Broadway, in which the zenith of cinematic glory has come spectacularly unstuck, evokes other spaces in which all-consuming visual ambition was devised but then overturned, leaving behind a condition of ruination all the more intensive, as in the gutted interior of the Rialto cinema, in that the space was originally envisaged as one of extreme splendour, and as the originating point for fascinations with sex, wealth or domination. Those spaces resonate globally and across time, with such entities as the erased Death Valley ghost-town of Ryan, or Hitler's Wolf's Lair war headquarters in Gierłoż, Poland. The interiors of the Broadway cinemas often emanate a sense that their exposure to reversal, from luxury to dereliction, was inbuilt at their conception, and that their prescient architects, such as S. Charles Lee, instilled within them a volatile charge of cinematic excess, with the explicit intention that it would, at some point in the future, be overturned so completely that the distinctive momentum of that reversal would generate new visual and architectural forms in which such pairings as opulence and fragmentation, or obsessive visual power and its capricious erasure, would be simultaneously evident. Even the naming of Hollywood's genres, such as 'film noir', evokes such wilfully self-cancelling pairings, in which the filmic will to see is integrally meshed with its darkening and annulling.

The ruined cinemas of Broadway form extraordinary apertures into the past history of film – as a history in which film's glamour and extravagance often appear to have possessed a consuming desire for their own cancellation – as well as into the future of visual media. In many ways, the terminal dereliction of cinematic space imbues a negative prognosis into that future, at film's end, as though that digitized future may be subject to perpetual, chronic malfunction. Since film always worked to embed itself profoundly into human vision, through its century or more of intimate inhabitation of all processes of behaviour and perception, its end implies the potential implanting of an incurable filmic disease, located at the very core of the eye, so that the formulation of post-filmic media may involve a process of projection by which that ingrained malfunction spectacularly projects itself outwards, entailing the imprintation into urban environments of the vital residue of the glorious scar of film. Film had an enduring preoccupation with such moments of catastrophic revelation – it often interrogated the ways in which a covert psychosis, once glaringly brought to light, could not then be extinguished, and also tracked the ways in which an alien and dangerous entity, concealed deep within a body, eventually worked its way to the surface, unleashing horror, by creating an opening which subsequently remained irreparably gaping.

If film forms a potential source of future maledictions, in the phantasmatic and disruptive forms it may take, it also exacts a set of demands upon its future spectators, in the work of delineating the arenas of vision and memory within which it will deploy itself. In that sense, the abandoned cinemas of Broadway, engrained with their own intricate strata of vision and memory, appear to possess an afterlife extending far beyond that of simply archiving film's residual detritus and its multiple ruination. In such cinemas, especially those from which the projection equipment, seating and all spatial orientation are long vanished, it often seems that their role as spaces intended for the habitual projection of films to spectators had been conceived only as an incidental afterthought, and that any omniscient onlooker, dispassionately observing the human species and its activities, might now perceive only the most tangential of connections between those spaces and the industrial consumption of film; instead, those cinemas' pre-eminent purpose, in their abandonment, might appear instead as that of constituting laboratories of vision (like Dr Chew's Eye World, in *Blade Runner*), in which seminal confrontations – such as that between film's terminal moments and the future media in which film remains embedded – form a focus of vital experimentation.

Film's Architectural Target-Practice

A distinctive architecture emerges from film's end that exists to project the pairings – between opulence and abandonment, between vision and its cancellation – which are integral to film's terminal moments and its future reinventions. Film and architecture themselves always constituted a volatile pairing, with film's extravagance envisioning the construction of immense architectural sets, either imagined or else based upon actual buildings, and architecture responding to film's obsessional spatial expansions by generating film-preoccupied environments that permeated entire cities associated with film, such as Los Angeles, Rome and Tokyo. As Giuliana Bruno notes, that contagious oscillation between film and architecture became embedded so deeply into urban landscape that it formed 'a creation of its filmic incarnations, for these, too, become part of its geography'.[3] Film's end exacerbates that process of oscillation, and transforms the inhabitant of film-haunted cities into the sensitized intermediator between film's residues and architecture's configurations, so that, in its vanishing, film aberrantly becomes architecturally pervasive, its charge of memory and obsession transmitted into awry architectural visions. While colossal cinemas of the 1920s and '30s, such as the Roxy in New York, and multiply focused cinematic spaces such as Broadway's Los Angeles Theater, voraciously assimilated all architectural elements into themselves, the dereliction or erasure of those cinemas generates an inverse process by which architectural space itself is overhauled and negatively inflected by film's abandonment, its constructions determined by film's disappearance.

The Hollywood and Highland Center, opened in 2001 on Hollywood Boulevard in Los Angeles after three years of construction, comprises a phantasmatic architectural emanation of film's dereliction and absence, composed in part from digital image-screens and elements drawn from the habitual forms of colossal shopping malls, together with a reapparition, forming the complex's architectural infrastructure, of the reconstruction, for D. W. Griffith's film Intolerance (1916), of the gates of Babylon, ready for their fall (the original set, in its grandiose redundancy, was relocated after the film's completion, to be prominently displayed at a Hollywood intersection, before being abandoned and left to deteriorate until its demolition in 1919, so that its contemporary architectural resuscitation emerges directly from that process of disintegration, rather than from its filmic glory). Embedded into the complex's facades and walkways, fragments of texts and images in the form of mosaics recount the 'bad histories' of Hollywood and of its industrial personnel's disillusionments. The complex's sprawling periphery swallows the Chinese Theater, one of the Hollywood Boulevard cinemas whose pre-eminence, as sites for film premieres, skewed the filmic configuration of Los Angeles westwards in the 1930s and led to the status of Broadway's lavish cinemas becoming overturned, rendering those cinemas increasingly neglected sites.

Up close, in the Hollywood and Highland Center, the malediction of film's residual memory, at its end, appears omnipresent, infiltrating the film-industry's spatial 'heart' in Hollywood, and unsettling that space's corporate architectural surfaces.

Drawing further back and upwards to the vantage-point of Mulholland Drive, the architecture of Hollywood, together with that of the entirety of Los Angeles, appears to carry that same destabilizing infiltration by film's memory and abandonment. Spectacular extravagance and its annulling remain irresolubly meshed, as though a film-derived intimacy with architectural forms, originating in the most minuscule, close-up detail of an abandoned cinema's fractured facade, or of the deteriorated Mayan-tiled concrete walls of Frank Lloyd Wright's Ennis House in the Los Feliz district (an enhanced variant of which Deckard inhabits in *Blade Runner*), may extend all the way outwards to an all-enveloping perspective that can take in the city's entire architectural expanse without any loss of film's inflexible, aberrant power as the determinant of that space. The future impact upon architecture of the residues of film, alongside other visual media, may generate forms in which a component inhabited by filmic memory and dereliction increases exponentially, while film's status as an active medium diminishes and entirely vanishes, so that all future architectural forms may finally devote themselves to a comprehensive embodiment of the multiple facets of film's ruination, and to a resuscitation of cinematic architecture that devotedly preserves intact film's vital collapse into abandonment.

While film often incorporated seductive architectural extravagance, such as that of New York in Fritz Lang's *Metropolis* (1927), and of Bangkok, and other East Asian megalopolises, in Wong Kar-Wai's *2046* (2004), it could also treat architecture with derision, even conceiving of itself as an attack upon architecture. Alongside a cinematic architecture which appears to wryly negate itself, as with that of the corrugated tin-can Rio cinema on the Bohemian

Highway, film may actively deride architecture as the embodiment of historical or political forces which endanger the filmmaker's survival. In Kurt Kren's *Window Gazers, Rubbish etc* (1962), the film-camera aggressively scans and targets Vienna's facades to locate gaping figures who use their building's windows as apertures from which to obliviously observe, and thereby approve, the actions in the street below, even when such actions may extend to the maltreatment, deportation and extermination of elements of Vienna's population: actions which, two decades earlier, had imperilled Kren himself. His declared intention, in filmically overturning processes of surveillance, was 'to shoot the people with the camera for looking out of the window'.[4] Architecture constitutes the protective screen for a malign ocular complicity with subjugation, which Kren's film must retrospectively attempt to assault, and to blind, using a strategy of extremely rapid editing and the overlayering of images, as a variant of the innumerable attacks upon the eye which proved invaluable to film's experiments and aims, throughout its history. For Kren, in 'shooting', film both creates images and violently rectifies the eye. Within contemporary architectural environments, the digital now takes on a parallel, all-engulfing project – of embodying oblivion – of the kind that Kren attacked, through film's perverse medium.

Window Gazers, Rubbish etc., 1962.

Film's Suturings

In 1995, around the centenary of the first cinema projections, preoccupations with film amassed around the concern that its autonomy as a medium was now obsolete, and that it needed to be expanded in new directions, or else would be subsumed and consumed by the digital. Filmmakers attracted by innovations in digital image-making, such as Greenaway and Wenders, explored ways in which those two futures of film could be combined. Almost twenty years earlier, in the final sequence of Wenders' elegiac road-movie *Kings of the Road* (1976), a forlorn cinema proprietor in rural Germany announces her intention to maintain her cinema in suspended abandonment, with the projectors poised in readiness, but showing no films to spectators, since the films habitually distributed to such cinemas (pornographic films) do not merit being shown; the film's last shot scans voided glass cabinets for forthcoming attractions, and the cinema's near-blown-out neon marquee. Looking into the future, Wenders' subsequent, spatially global film, *Until the End of the World* (1991) – whose in-transit characters lose and relocate a mysterious memory-recording device as they travel from continent to continent – had envisaged digital image-making as possessing the potential for the salutary rectification of an act of blinding: an act which film had always compulsively interrogated and, in extreme cases such as that of Kren, advocated and perpetrated, as a response to visually oriented political subjugation and surveillance. The anatomizings and woundings of the eye that had, in their multiple forms, been a preoccupation of film, then appeared to be entirely discarded in the years following film's centenary; a vastly accelerated and incessant proliferation of the digital derisively cast aside those filmmakers' aspirations for a reflective, exploratory combining of the filmic with the digital, intended to generate a future healing of human vision, after the traumas it had undergone

Kings of the Road,
1976.

throughout the twentieth century. The eye, within digital power, then became a focus of oblivion, neither subject to exploratory woundings, nor conceived as a healable organ, but instead solely constituting a complicit vessel whose activity was to absorb and re-transmit data. Digital environments relentlessly generated datapanics, sensory and economic meltdowns, and annullings of human experience, while dissolving the distinctive forms of cities; above all, digital environments foreclosed the very idea of 'the end', since their power conceived of itself as integrally endless: ongoing, subject to exacerbation, intensification, proliferation, but never to a process of closure, like that towards which film was always capriciously ready to abandon itself, together with its spectacular glory, thereby rendering itself into filmic fragments and traces.

The loss of the end entails a separation from the bliss and elation which filmic abandonment may entail. Even when a film ended abruptly and in calamity, as with Hitchcock's *Vertigo*, that tearing-away of the spectator's attention from the sudden horror of Judy's plunge into death from the San Juan Bautista mission's tower, made definitive by the last film-image's fade-out, remains infused with

Until the End of the World, 1991 (memories).

the extraordinary sensory journey, of revelation and obsession, taken to that moment, so that the film's memory irresistibly bursts through its durational ending, and begins to configure an intricate post-filmic entity in a more mutable zone of memorial time and space, in which the spectator is intimately 'haunted' by the film, or by isolated images within it. Hollywood's genre-films habitually possessed such clearcut trajectories towards their ending that their audiences could derive a different form of terminal experience, of anticipating and then inhabiting the assuredness of that final moment. Even a spectator of the disintegrating Broadway cinemas, during the era in which they projected last-ditch exploitation or pornographic films, moved through a tangible boundary, holding tion, before that spectator was then expelled into the raw urban environment. A filmic end disparately created ecstasies, banal pleasures or traversals, but always impacted upon its spectator's senses.

Whenever a film's celluloid snapped mid-projection, the projection-box would be transformed from an atmosphere of calm to uproar, with an abrupt speeding-up of time, since every lost second counted, and the uproar worsened, before the projection process could be re-established; especially during all-night cult-film

Vertigo, 1958.

screenings, in Broadway's cinemas of the 1970s, that moment carried optimal risk for the screen, whose surface would be indented from missiles thrown by impatient, addled spectators, and also for the vulnerable infrastructure of once-lavish cinematic space (illuminated in all of its shameful, denuded decay, since a break in projection always activated the auditorium's house lights). The suturing process habitually involved the film-reel being manually transported from the projector to an adjoining table, and laid out, as though for an express autopsy, its damage scanned with devoted concentration by the projectionist. Then, with adroit rapidity, the rip was spliced. Once the film's resuscitation had been verified, with the reactivation of the projector, renewed darkness, and the first image's apparition on the now-stained, serrated screen, that suturing of the malfunctioned medium invariably precipitated an extreme corporeal response: cries, applause, screams, before a new captivation within film.

The already 'broken' digital world, its power only several decades old in contrast with that of film, but now malfunctioned beyond repair through its regime of human jettisoning, corporate meltdown, accelerating viral furore and catastrophic data-collapse, may now require a similar operation of last-ditch suturing through the intervention of film. But rather than needing only the careful application of an emergency splice to reactivate its non-material form, the digital instead demands a fundamental overhaul which would re-orient its 'endlessness' towards the suspended abandonment of film and of cinematic space, so that the work of digital technologies could be entirely devoted, with a dedication equivalent to that of die-hard cinema-projectionists, to the sustaining and archiving of film's infinite memory. The painstaking process of the suturing and re-splicing of the digital world through film would then absorb and consume those two media within one another, thereby liberating the human eye to explore new visions and endings.

Indestructible Films

At that moment of long-lost preoccupation with the ending or 'death' of cinema, coinciding with the centenary of 1895's first projections of films for paying audiences (a moment which now appears to contain as much strangely misguided foresight about the future of visual media as that of a century earlier), an idea promoting the relinquishment of film's power into decay and disappearance viewed film as having run its natural course. Similarly, at that moment, when the immediacy of cinematic closures had yet to settle into a durational form of abandonment (in 1995, the last functioning cinemas of Los Angeles's Broadway were only just lapsing from exploitation-genre and pornographic film-projection into dereliction), it appeared, as a correspondingly natural event, that spaces designed with lavish extravagance in a vanished era could no longer exert a hold on contemporary environments, and needed to fade out, or submit to their spatial transformation into plasma-television storerooms or other recyclings. In that sense, film's fall was perceived as linear progress towards the attaining of a threshold, after which it would be destroyed or consumed within time, as a process of organic deterioration, existing in tension with film's own insurgent destructivity, as an instrument conceived, in its experimental or revolutionary forms, for assaults upon human vision and power-formations, or against time itself.

Alternatively, film could subsist, as though possessing the annulled status of colonized territories whose rulers, such as those absorbed by imperial Rome or Britain, offered an open acknowledgement of their subjugation in order to maintain an artifice of residual power. In that sense, the words 'film' and 'cinema', when understood within the language of an era of engulfing digital media, would still resonate, and even indicate events in which image-sequences were transmitted for spectators within enclosed spaces; but whatever had previously made film a vivifying compulsion, and a distinctive entity that generated memory and dreams, had gone. In Wenders' *Until the End of the World*, the mysterious device which supplants film, and is programmed to seize memories, thereby healing blindness, eventually misfires by exhausting and excoriating the eyes of the woman (the mother of the device's operator) for whom it is intended to the point of precipitating her death; that same technology for seizing memories is then adapted into one for the recording and projection of dreams, but again it misfires, leading to maleficent and painful addictions, fixated upon pixellated dream-images, on the part of its users, who either die, or (as with the dream-agent Claire) leave the planet behind in order to gaze down upon it from the portal of a spaceship, in bliss and elation, as though finally watching a film. Film always formed a capricious medium, from its initial conjuring in the hands of magician-tricksters. Constrictive formations for film's deployment – extending from those of Hollywood's film industries, which managed only a relatively brief moment of glory before crashing down, as though impelled by self-destructivity, to those of contemporary digital industries, into

Until the End of the World, 1991 (dreams).

which film is obliviously subsumed, thereby constituting a non-complicit entity which only serves to exacerbate catastrophic digital crashes – appear always to malfunction, as though such formations are fatally antithetical to film's vital experiments.

Film's own indestructible images often emerge from a fragile process in which the human eye searches, through the intervention of film and as an integral element of a filmmaker's journey which may be ended at any moment, for images of itself: images which illuminate, and reveal, the origination and projection of vision, even when the environment within which those images are located is one of incipient blindness or death, from which light may imminently be voided. In Chris Marker's film *Sunless* a cinematographer incessantly travels between continents, acutely aware, notably during his inhabitation of Tokyo, of the potential mutation beyond film, into a technological domain he calls 'the Zone', of the images he is seizing with his film-camera. Marker's Vertov-impelled cinematographer is preoccupied with the impossible rendering into film of memories and dreams, but above all, with film's work as an inexhaustible archiving of the intricate gestures and insights of human vision.

Future visual media may be improvised from aberrant amalgams of images that incorporate alliances with film's ineradicable residues, instead of emerging from systematized, industrial formations. Similarly, the interiors of abandoned cinemas, such as those of Broadway, may hold – especially in their most intensified conditions of ruination, or their most radical shifts into opposed re-usages – elements of an indestructibility of cinematic space that emerges when those interiors appear to be so comprehensively sieved out of all habitual perceptions of cinematic space, constituting extreme states of dereliction or transformation, that they abruptly resurge as pivotal sites for the origination of unprecedented visual forms. In that sense, the accumulated strata of debris and the jaggedly ripped apart screens of auditoria such as that of the Rialto cinema, and the unleashing of vocal glossolalia within once-opulent cinemas turned into densely populated cultist-churches, such as the State cinema, together amass raw material for a future moment when the act of cinematic projection itself may be reconceived.

Sunless, 1982.

Film's Tricksters

The work of the magician-pioneers present at film's origins, above all that of the Skladanowsky Brothers in Berlin and Georges Méliès in Paris, forms an illumination of such processes as the future reconception of the projection of images. Those pioneer figures themselves inhabited an era in intimate proximity to one in which film's status was non-existent – or else had been in the process of preparatory formulation, combining phantasmatic pre-filmic spectacles with photographic experiments on corporeal image-sequences, such as those of Muybridge. The extreme points which define and also annul film's history – the instant before film came into being, and the instant after film ceased – are bound together; if film is able to traverse that terminal boundary, as a ghostly seep-age of images and spatial inhabitations, it now survives in a pro-foundly mutated state, disruptively infiltrating its resuscitated configuration into contemporary visual media forms. Even at its origin, film was already invested with horrifying ghost-traces and corporeal obsessions, and with an intractable mystery about the nature of image-projection, as it is at film's end. That irresoluble enigma surrounding film projection, which initially defied the capacities of even the most adroit magician-pioneers (together with their more scientifically oriented counterparts, such as Louis Le Prince), eventually embedded itself within the unwieldy tech-nologies adopted for the standardized projection of film-celluloid, which always conveyed a sense that films were somehow being projected wrongly, as though through a deeply mismatched, haz-ardous medium, thereby exacting unremitting concentration from their projectionists. The contemporary projections of visual media, via digital image-screens and other surfaces, carry an identical aura of intrinsic malfunction, indicating that a re-conception of the projection of images now needs to be formulated from zero, primarily though an exploration of the multiple strategies envisioned by film's originating tricksters.

Tricksters always operate through a vertiginous process of visual deceit, by creating a sleight of the eye which makes their spectators' vision reel, so that something is perceived in the place of an actual absence: an act always integral to film's material-conjurations, from light, darkness and movement. The Skladanowsky Brothers slyly undertook the greatest of all deceptions within film's history, and as its first act, by making the audience for their programme at the Wintergarten ballroom in Berlin in November 1895 pay for admission to the experience of film, in the form of a screening (initially, a wild success), programmed at the conclusion of a variety performance, and consisting of nine six-second films, repeated over a duration of fifteen minutes, projected onto the rear of the screen, and using a dual-projector system known as a 'Bioskop'. Every subsequent occurrence of cinematic abandonment, and of film's dereliction, is indissolubly welded to that originating moment of trickery, since, in all abandoned cinemas, such as those of Los Angeles's Broadway, the proprietors' decision, on closure, resulted from an inverse moment: the absence of a paying audience. Film always worked to defer its spectators' pleasures in order to intensify them, by finally delivering a particular sensorial impact; similarly, that first public act of cinematic projection finally precipitated (after a century or more of deferral) film's abandonment, together with the elations and resuscitations surrounding that terminal moment.

The work of the magician-tricksters at film's origins generates film's end, and also reveals the volatile dynamics of that end-point, just as the mutability of the ruined cinemas of Broadway, which enables their interiors' abrupt transformations into cultist-churches or nightclubs, is illuminated by the Skladanowsky Brothers' own capacity to conjure the pre-existing space of an entertainment ballroom in Berlin, over several weeks in 1895, into an unprecedented entity: a 'cinema'. Interrogating the residues of film implies the resuscitation, for contemporary visual media, of the perverse preoccupations of those magician-pioneers, whose compulsion to create film resulted from their trickster-capacities to elude fixed conceptions of time and space, to provoke outrage and laughter, to perpetrate image-thievery and deception (among themselves, first of all), and to assume the form of vanishing shape-shifters who, once their essential work was done, decided, as though by caprice, or as the result of a sudden fall from grace, to abandon the domain of film, and return to that of magic (an exit filmically visualized in Georges Franju's documentary, *Le Grand Méliès*, 1952, in which Franju displays the shabby cabinet on a Parisian railway station where the impoverished Méliès sold magic tricks to children in his post-filmic life). To disappear from film, as Méliès and the Skladanowsky Brothers did, as an act of terminal conjuration, constitutes as seminal and aberrant a form of visual power as that of a derelict cinema, suspended in a state of abandonment, when it miraculously rematerializes the experience of film.

Cinematic Abandonment and The End

The night of the once-yearly film-projection at the Los Angeles Theater took place in intense heat, with a jagged line of wildfires visible far to the north, high up on the sheer inclines of the San Gabriel mountain range, where cinematic projections had once been held in the casino of a luxurious resort-complex, built as an act of insanity in that hostile environment at the summit of Echo Mountain. Precariously reached by a mountain railway and cable-car, it was maintained in operation only for a period of several months before that improvised cinema was swept away and propelled as debris down the mountainside, along with the entire resort-complex and the railway, in one night of terrible flash-floods and lightning fires in 1905, leaving behind only bare fragments of foundations, visible over a century later among the long-abandoned ruins as the enduring trace of an obsession, against all odds, to project films. On that night on Broadway, the smell of smoke from the wildfires intimated that the conflagration could effortlessly encompass the entire megalopolis. A crowd had gathered outside the Los Angeles Theater, waiting on the pavement's expanse of fractured terrazzo tiles, whose icons of tiny golden flames appeared to resonate from the wildfires surmounting the megalopolis. That crowd amassed like the one that had awaited the cinema's lavish opening night, and had included Chaplin and Albert Einstein; but, instead of being avidly impelled to that site by the irresistible glory of film's industries, and its contrast with America's misery, as in January 1931, the curious clientele awaiting the projection appeared drawn by the attraction of a unique or terminal event (although the yearly film-screenings had endured for more than a decade, part of the cinema's building was now earmarked for transformation into 'live-work' apartments, generating the possibility that this screening would be the very last). In the uproar of night-time Broadway,

Gentlemen Prefer Blondes, 1953.

its desperate, derelict inhabitants were cajoling or threatening one another for low-value coins, but the white-bearded, aged ex-projectionist who habitually haunted that terrazzo pavement, holding his shaking styrofoam cup, was nowhere to be seen, as though, when a film was finally to be materialized in that cinema, he had been dutifully compelled, like other ephemeral conjurors of vision such as Méliès and the Skladanowsky Brothers, to vanish away.

At the top of the spiral staircase accessed from the rear of the highest balcony of the Los Angeles Theater, the projection-box had fallen into a last-minute panic; the two projectors, despite their meticulous preparation, over a period of several months, in anticipation of this moment by the filmic die-hard who also maintained California's other surviving film-projectors, from the Fremont cinema in San Luis Obispo to the Rio cinema on the Bohemian Highway, appeared ready to malfunction. Once brought back to life, those vast projectors grated and protested, as though wrenched from the coma of their suspended abandonment, but also volubly strained by their overheating, in that barely ventilated space that threatened to spark its own engulfing ignition, as though to form the last historical instance among the innumerable cinematic conflagrations which had begun in 1896, only shortly after the originating filmic spectacles, and had accumulated into an archive of cinematic death by fire. The film to be projected was still being assembled from its battered cans, and the filmic die-hard and his fraught assistant focused on the last minutes before the screening began, urgently communicating and cursing to one another in the technical vocabulary of cinematic projection, which now formed a peripheral or endangered language of the film-compelled human species.

Through the projection-box window, the cinema's seats could be seen filling, in front of the exposed screen, for the first time in a year, constituting an aberrant spectacle, since, with the exceptions of the auditoria of those of Broadway's cinemas now transformed

Los Angeles Theater facade.

into cultist churches, the interiors of those cinemas always appeared as voided zones from which all human presence had been exclud-ed in order to allow the crucial processes of cinematic ruination to deepen, and perform their work, in generating fragments of filmic memory and phantasmatic cinema-hauntings. As with the experi-ence of gutted or mutated cinemas, such as the Globe, in which all spatial orientation had become blurred and lost, with the screen and projection-box long gone, it now appeared a perverse occupation of those spectators to inhabit the auditorium, as though all connec-tion between cinematic space and its audiences had become irrepar-ably lost, for any detached onlooker, at the point when abandoned cinemas, after their closure as venues for pornographic or exploi-tation-genre films, had assumed their new mission as experimental laboratories for new configurations of human vision. Traversing the labyrinthine domain of the Los Angeles Theater, with its multi-ple points of focus – its lounge, restaurant, marble restrooms, children's playroom, fountain, and Versailles-inspired palatial foyer – those spectators undertook an archaeological excavation of cine-matic space's debris.

Abruptly, before everyone had taken their seats, the projector activated the first film-image, which crossed the dust-swirled expanse of space from the projection-box to the screen in a fraction of an instant, while the cinema's sound-system, as decrepit as its projectors but overhauled with an equivalent care, suddenly roared into cacophony, as though the synchronization of image and sound had been achieved through sheer improvisation, rather than con-stituting the all-powerful film-industrial alliance which had notoriously terminated the 1920s work of image-focused experi-mental filmmakers. The audience now appeared entranced and unrestrained, many weeping, or laughing. In its sensorial trans-porting, film seemed unstoppable, unendable. From the very back of the highest balcony, at the foot of the spiral staircase which led

to the projection-box, the entire mass of that film-vivified audience
appeared in stark contrast to the cinema's interior, now poised at the
boundary between last-ditch magnificence and denuded ruination;
the deteriorating angels and cherubs, decorating the ornate columns
and balconies at either side of the auditorium, seemed terminally
decayed and disgraced, and the once-sumptuous golden ceiling's
medallions appeared still more intricately fissured and water-
damaged than when the cinema had been emptied out. Instead of
being resuscitated by its spectators' presence, the cinema instead
had now entered more profoundly into dereliction – its form embodying an exacerbated, extreme status of abandonment – as a
result of that momentary human inhabitation, and its now-immi-
nent withdrawal, as the projected film entered its final sequence.

Moments before the end of the projection, I left the auditorium of the Los Angeles Theater behind, in order not to witness
that terminal abandoning of the cinema, and instead, to see it still
instantaneously ripped open, and lividly activated, as a site of film
– descending the lush, red-carpeted flights of stairs, past the
crystal fountain and through the extravagant, near-deserted lobby,
under its immense chandeliers, and out through the cinema's doors
and past the ticket kiosk, in which the proprietor was counting his
final takings, as the Skladanowsky Brothers must have done on the
night of the first public cinematic projection on 1 November 1895.
Back in the cinema's overheated auditorium, the rapt spectators
were experiencing and traversing the film's end; in the projection-
box, the last sequence of celluloid passed over the beam of light
which propelled the film-images towards the screen below, before
finally giving out, rattling around its reel, so that the projectionist
could finally breathe in relief, his work accomplished, and begin to
close down his vision-machines. Out in the heat of Broadway, the
contact with film's momentarily reactivated lavishness collided
wildly with the oncoming brutality of the haywire megalopolis's

night aura. On an end-to-end journey, through the seminal filmic detritus of Los Angeles's Broadway, from the United Artists cinema at its southernmost perimeter, to the Million Dollar Theater at its northern end, those unique cinemas intimate both film's vital abandonment, and film's insurgence into the future of human vision.

REFERENCES

Introduction

1 In this book, the term 'cinematic space' invariably refers to the visual, tangible space of cinemas as entities – their infrastructure, architecture, interiors and facades – rather than, as the term is sometimes used, the space depicted within individual film shots.

PART 1: Film and The End

1 Paulo Cherchi Usai, *The Death of Cinema: History, Cultural Memory and the Digital Dark Age* (London, 2001), p. 89.
2 Lev Manovich, *The Language of New Media* (Cambridge, MA, 2001), p. 55.
3 Usai, *The Death of Cinema*, p. 13.
4 Bill Morrison, notes for the DVD booklet, *Decasia: The State of Decay* (New York, 2005), p. 2.
5 Laura Mulvey, *Death 24x a Second: Stillness and the Moving Image* (London, 2005), p. 17.
6 Rebecca Solnit, *Motion Studies: Time, Space and Eadweard Muybridge* (London, 2003), p. 241.
7 Arthur Rimbaud, *Illuminations* (New York, 1946), p. xxvi.
8 Film's presence in Death Valley is documented in Hugh C. Tolford, *Take the Train to Death Valley* (Visalia, 2008).

9 Matthew Gandy, 'The Cinematic Void: Desert Iconographies in Michelangelo Antonioni's *Zabriskie Point*', in *Landscape and Film*, ed. Martin Lefebvre (New York, 2006), p. 324.
10 Giuliana Bruno, *Atlas of Emotion* (London, 2002), p. 48.

PART 2: Abandoned Images

1 The Million Dollar Theater's marquee is filmically caught in the original version of *Blade Runner* in two forms: as the replicant Pris reaches the Bradbury Building, the marquee across the avenue announces the film *El Siete Vidas* (1980), a low-budget Mexican crime drama directed by Jaime Fernández and featuring the popular actor Andrés Garcia, whose name appears prominently on the marquee, above the film's title; in all of its subsequent appearances, including J. F. Sebastian's arrival at the Bradbury Building, only filmic moments after Pris's arrival, the marquee announces not the screening of a film, but a concert, by a Chilean band, Los Mimilocos Mazacote y Orquestra. In the 'final cut' of *Blade Runner* (2007), this continuity error is digitally corrected, so that the second of the marquee variants appears in all shots.
2 Miriam Hansen, *Babel and Babylon: Spectatorship in American Silent Film* (Cambridge, MA, 1991), pp. 16 and 25.
3 Maurice Lemaître, *Has the Film Already Started?* (Paris, 1995), pp. 21 and 25.
4 Lauren Rabinovitz, 'From *Hale's Tours* to *Star Tours*: Virtual Voyages, Travel Ride Films, and the Delirium of the Hyper-real', in *Virtual Voyages: Cinema and Travel*, ed. Jeffrey Ruoff (Durham, NC, 2006), p. 42.
5 Maggie Valentine, *The Show Starts on the Sidewalk: An Architectural History of the Movie Theatre* (New Haven, CT, 1994), p. 27.
6 Francis Bacon, *The Brutality of Fact: Interviews with David Sylvester* (London, 1987), p. 200.

PART 3: Abandoned Eyes

1 Dziga Vertov, *Kino-Eye: The Writings of Dziga Vertov* (Berkeley, CA, 1984), pp. 14–15.
2 Ibid., pp. 67–8.
3 Antonin Artaud, 'Cinéma et Réalité', in *Oeuvres Complètes: III* (Paris, 1978), p. 19.
4 Maggie Valentine, *The Show Starts on the Sidewalk: An Architectural History of the Movie Theatre* (New Haven, CT, 1994), p. 62.

PART 4: Film and Film's End: Resuscitated Images

1 Mark Holborn, *Beyond Japan* (London, 1991), p. 39.
2 Brochure of the TDK Corporation History Museum (Akita, 2009), unpaginated.
3 Giuliana Bruno, *Atlas of Emotion* (London, 2002), p. 27.
4 Hans Scheugl, *Kurt Kren: Structural Films* (Vienna, 2005), p. 12. Kren left Vienna for Rotterdam in 1939, at the age of ten, as a Jewish child of the Kindertransport, and did not return to Vienna until 1947.

ACKNOWLEDGEMENTS

I'd like to thank the Rockefeller Foundation, and its Bellagio Study Centre, for inviting me to the Villa Serbelloni in Bellagio, Italy, where this book originated. I'd also like to thank the California Institute of the Arts, and especially its Dean of Critical Studies, Nancy Wood, for inviting me there as a visiting professor, and enabling this book to develop. I'm grateful to András Bereznay for his map of the cinemas of Broadway. Finally, I'd like to thank Oscar Arce (for invaluable help in Los Angeles), Anne Waldman, Matthew Gandy, Mark Shiel, Will Brooker, Nick Bradshaw and Gareth Evans.